CW00864413

ASPERGER SYNDROME, THE SWAN & THE BURGLAR

Brenda Boyd

authorHOUSE®

AuthorHouse™ UK Ltd.
500 Avebury Boulevard
Central Milton Keynes, MK9 2BE
www.authorhouse.co.uk
Phone: 08001974150

First published by AuthorHouse   5/3/2007

ISBN: 978-1-4343-1118-4 (sc)

Printed in the United States of America
Bloomington, Indiana

This book is printed on acid-free paper.

TABLE OF CONTENTS

Chapter 1

Trouble in School

Miss Neill stood at the front of the class. She was teaching long division.

'Right, children' she said. 'We've done enough examples. You can have a go on your own now'

At that, loud groans were to be heard throughout the class, together with comments like 'Oh, no!' and 'Have a heart, miss!' - Clearly long division was not their favourite topic!

But Miss Neill dismissed all objections with a wave of her hand.

'I want you to turn to page 17 and complete numbers 1 - 4'

Among the rustling of papers that followed, there were a good many heavy sighs, as the children settled down to do their work.

'And one more thing, children' said Miss Neill. 'There is to be **complete silence** while you work'

Ryan was sitting at the back of the class, a fair-haired boy who looked so much younger than the rest of the class that he almost seemed out of place. He was very bright really, but there were certain things that he had a problem with - and Miss Neill was one of them. There was something about her pale blubbery face and stinging comments that always made him think of a jellyfish.

Unfortunately for Ryan, another of his problems was paying attention in class! So he hadn't heard most of what

Miss Neill said. He did hear the words 'There is to be complete silence' though, and when he did so he smiled happily to himself. He liked it when the teacher said that, because every time she did, the classroom became lovely and calm, and he could relax for a while.

He had learned, though, that during these quiet times you could not just do what you liked. You had to 'toe the line'

Leaning back in his chair, Ryan thought about the first time Dad told him that in school he needed to toe the line - which brings us to another thing he had a problem with. You see, sometimes Ryan found it hard to understand what people meant, so he had pictured the classroom, wondering which line he would have to toe. It must be some line on the floor, he decided, if he was expected to put his toe against it - But which one? There were so many lines on the floor. But then Dad had explained.

'Toeing the line means you have to do what the teacher tells you to do – if you don't, you'll keep getting into trouble'.

'Trouble' was one thing Ryan did know about! So he knew he should 'toe the line' now.

The only problem was he hadn't a clue what he was supposed to be doing! Biting down hard on his lip, he watched the other children with their heads down, working away.

Suddenly he felt a tap on his arm.

'Ryan...' whispered Kev Shepherd 'Page 17, numbers 1-4'.

Kev Shepherd was the boy who sat next to Ryan, and

it's hard to imagine a less likely looking pair – Ryan so small and fair and Kev so tall, dark and heavy. It looked like there could have been four or five years age difference between the two of them.

Kev knew that Ryan was forever getting into trouble in school, and he didn't want it to happen again today. You see, Kev was a very nice boy. But unfortunately Ryan didn't realise this. (This was because of something else he was not very good at – judging who was nice and who was not) And so, without even thanking Kev, Ryan turned to page 17.

When he saw page 17, he was relieved. He had his calculator in his bag so he could do 1-4 in no time! And sure enough, within a few minutes he had all four answers neatly written out.

For a moment he sat back wondering why everyone else was so slow. Then with a shrug he started to cover the rest of the page with some work of his own – 'List Making' work, as he liked to call it.

Ryan, as you can already see, was an unusual boy in a lot of ways. So you won't be surprised to learn that he had an unusual hobby too - which was making lists, of all things! In his spare time there was nothing he loved to do more than writing lists about things that he was interested in - All sorts of lists: types of dinosaurs, breeds of dog, film titles, telephone numbers. Any time Ryan took an interest in something, he liked to learn all he could and write lists about it. And he had a fantastic memory for everything he had learned.

Before long the rest of his page was covered with rows of addresses, written in his messy handwriting (or 'scrawl' as Miss Neill liked to call it). He intended to copy these into his 'Address List' when he got home later. And so, as the rest of the class struggled over their long division, Ryan was working away happily, in a world of his own.

Unfortunately he didn't notice Miss Neill as she stood with her arms folded, calling his name in a cross tone of voice.

The other children looked up. This promised to be more fun than long division.

A few moments later, she called his name again – louder this time - but still he didn't hear it. He was completing a list of addresses from one side of a street near where he lived.

'49, Belmont Crescent' he wrote. Then
'51, Belmont Crescent'

By this stage the entire class had stopped work to watch. All eyes were on Ryan as Miss Neill called his name again. Very loudly this time!

'RYAN GILLESPIE!' she yelled.

Ryan looked up with a start. Why had she shouted so loud? He hated it when she did that. It usually meant he was in trouble. He quickly turned over his work so no one could see.

'Ryan' said Miss Neill quietly 'now that we have your attention, would you care to tell the class what *exactly* you are doing?' she asked.

Ryan quickly tried to size up the situation in his mind. He thought she seemed to be talking very politely.

'Maybe I'm not in trouble after all' he said to himself. 'I mean, she's not *insisting* I tell. She's giving me a choice by asking if I *care* to'

'No' he muttered gruffly.

'What do you mean NO?'

'No, I wouldn't care to' he said.

Miss Neill marched straight to his desk. She turned over his work and made a sort of snorting noise when she saw the list of addresses, written below the correct answers to numbers 1-4.

'So you thought it would be smart to use a calculator, did you?' asked Miss Neill.

'Yes' he replied.

There was a silence for a few moments. Ryan still wasn't sure if he was in trouble or not. He had done the sums after all.

'Tell me this' said Miss Neill. 'Which one of us do you think is smarter? Me or you?'

Ryan didn't know what to say.

What a weird question, he thought. He knew *he* was very smart, because his Mum was forever going on about it. *'You're such a bright boy, Ryan'* she would moan. *'If only you'd learn to behave'.* But how on earth was he supposed to know how smart his teacher was? He struggled to think of an answer that might make her happy.

'Well, I suppose you *could* be smarter than me,' he replied, smiling hopefully. 'You are pretty old, after all'

From the roars of laughter around the class, it was obvious to Ryan that he had said something funny. He wasn't sure what. He just knew he hated it when the other children laughed at him like that. But he was completely taken aback when Miss Neill began to yell at him as well.

'GET OUT OF MY CLASS! NOW! Straight to the Headmaster's office. I'm not putting up with any more of your cheek'

All the way to the headmaster's office, Ryan dragged his heels. He didn't know what he had done wrong this time - just that he was in trouble again. For only last week Mr Stevenson, the headmaster had given him a lecture about his 'unacceptable attitude.' And before he sent him on his way he had said

'I'd better not see you in here again, Ryan or there will be trouble'

Not only that, but Mum had threatened him when he got home.

'If you end up in the headmaster's office one more time' she had yelled, 'you're really going to get it!'

Ryan wondered what she meant by *you're really going to get it*. She didn't explain what *it* was, so he didn't know *what* he was going to get. But Mum was yelling so much he was scared to ask. He just knew that *it* must be something very bad. And unfortunately Mum always found out about trouble in school, because Ryan's twin brother, Danny loved to tell her - which was one of the many things Ryan hated about having a twin in his class.

'Not you again, Ryan' Mr Stevenson said, when he saw him in his office. But then, in response to every question he was asked, Ryan stared at the floor and said nothing. Mr Stevenson was not surprised at this. Because although Ryan's parents had told him that at home Ryan could be very lively and talkative, at school he rarely said more than a few words. As a result, Mr Stevenson had to find out from Miss Neill what had gone on.

But when Miss Neill joined them, Ryan still didn't speak - though I have to tell you he didn't listen much either. There wasn't much point. The headmaster rarely said anything new or interesting, and today's lecture seemed just as boring as last week's. So Ryan just stood there, trying hard not to burst into tears and rush out of the room.

As you might guess, Ryan had his own special method of dealing with difficult situations like this. It was one that no one in the world knew about or would even have suspected. He called it 'Tooth Tapping', and it was a method he had invented all by himself when he was very small - quite by accident!

It came about once when Dad told him a good way to stay out of trouble.

'Just keep your tongue in your cheek' he had advised.

Then later Mum gave him a different suggestion, so he was a bit confused.

'Try counting to 10' she had said.

The next time that Ryan was upset, he tried Dad's idea first, but found it impossible to keep his tongue in one place inside his cheek. Even if he did manage it for a moment, it was then impossible to count aloud. So he devised a way of tapping each tooth in turn with his tongue, silently allocating each one a number.

In Ryan's mind, Tooth Tapping was a good way of using both Mum's and Dad's ideas at the same time! Often in school, during times when he was supposed to be paying attention or getting on with work, instead Ryan would be working out number patterns in his head, by tapping each tooth in a particular order. Which is exactly what he was doing in the headmaster's office that afternoon, while he and Miss Neill droned on and on.

'I hope you're listening, young man' barked Mr Stevenson suddenly.

'Better try and listen for a bit' Ryan thought to himself. So he nodded.

'I will have to speak to your parents again. We will not tolerate defiance and cheek in this school'

Ryan continued to stare at the floor.

'Miss Neill, before I let this young man go,' the headmaster continued 'is there anything you'd like to add?'

Miss Neill gave one of her snorts.

'I'm not sure there's any point, when he hasn't even got the manners to answer' she said. 'But Ryan, you really *must* make more effort from now on. Are you prepared to do that?'

Ryan hadn't realised it was rude not to reply. He certainly didn't *intend* to be rude.

'OK' he muttered.

'Well, I just hope you mean it' Miss Neill went on. 'And if I was to give you one piece of advice to help you stay out of trouble, it would be this. Try to be a bit more like your brother, Danny'

Ryan studied her for a moment, puzzled. Maybe she wasn't so smart after all, he thought. How could she not have noticed? He was small and fair. Danny was tall and dark. Did Miss Neill really think he could grow six inches and make his hair darker - just by trying?

'That would be an extremely silly thing to try' he explained patiently. 'You see, Danny and I are non-identical twins'

Chapter 2

THREATS & LIES

Dad was fed up listening to the twins arguing. He knew from the moment he picked them up from school that they were going to be difficult. They argued even more than usual about who would sit in the front of the car, so in the end he told them both to sit in the back and put up with it!

'Why do you have to be such a freak anyway?' asked Danny in a vicious tone.

'I'm not a freak!' Ryan yelled.

'You are. Everyone knows you are. Dad, it's not fair. I hate being in the same class as him'

'I hate it too!' said Ryan with a passion.

'No wonder you've got no friends, freak'

'Danny, that's enough. Don't speak to your brother like that' said Dad with a warning tone in his voice.

'But Dad, he was messing around in class today again. It's so embarrassing. I hate being the freak's twin'

Dad pulled over, switched off the engine and turned round to face them. He was a huge bear of a man with dark hair and a bristly beard, but, as Mum often said, he was really just a 'gentle giant' who rarely even raised his voice. On this occasion however spoke very sternly.

'I'm telling you, Danny. That's enough! Now I don't want another word from either of you till we get home'

So they were both quiet for a while - which Ryan was glad of because, as you know, he loved silence. He settled down to look out the window.

'Freak!' hissed Danny under his breath.

Ryan just ignored him.

When at last the car pulled up outside the house, Dad turned round to them again.

'Danny, you've had plenty of time to cool off now. Is there anything you'd like to say to your brother?'

What he hoping to hear, of course was an apology.

'Just that I'm going to kill him' replied Danny. And with that he jumped out of the car and raced to the house.

So for the moment Dad gave up trying to make peace. He sent each of the boys to their rooms as a punishment - Ryan for getting into trouble in school and Danny for being mean to Ryan. Danny hated the punishment but Ryan didn't mind at all. He just settled down quietly and got on with his Address List.

After a while Dad looked into Ryan's room. Ryan didn't even look up.

'You OK, Ryan?'

'Yeah'

'I've just been on the phone to the school'

'Oh?'

'What went wrong today then, son?' he asked gently.

'Dunno'

Dad stared at the top of his son's blonde head. He had just spent fifteen minutes listening to the school's latest complaints – Ryan was rude to other children. Ryan refused to comply. Ryan wouldn't do his work. Ryan was cheeky to teachers. But even though Dad had heard it all before, he didn't feel angry. Somehow he knew Ryan didn't mean any harm.

'Your mother's not going to be best pleased, you know' he said gently.

Ryan looked up when he heard that.

'What will she do to me?'

'Don't worry, son. I'll have a word with her'

Later on Maria put her head round the door as well. Maria was Danny and Ryan's big sister. There were only three children in the Gillespie family, though in Ryan's view Maria was nearly an adult, because she was almost sixteen. And, as Mum often said, when she was dressed up, she would pass for twenty! With her dark colouring and tall slender figure, it seemed she had taken after her Dad in every way. Ryan liked Maria. She was one of those people who got on well with everyone really.

'Hi Ryan' she said. 'You in trouble in school again?'

'Yeah…. And Danny says I'm a freak'

'You're not a freak. Don't worry'

'I hate Danny'

'You don't really'

'I do. And he hates me'

'He doesn't really'

'He does. He said he is going to kill me'

'Ryan, he doesn't *mean* that'

'He does. And I hate school as well'

'It can't be all that bad surely'

'It is. Ryan has stacks of friends and they all hate me too'

'Then make some friends of your own' she said.

Ryan looked puzzled.

'Seriously' she went on. 'Why don't you try being more friendly in school'

Ryan thought about it for a moment.

'Go on' she coaxed. 'Will you give it a go?'

'Maybe' said Ryan.

When Mum came home, she told Ryan that she and Dad needed to have a 'serious talk' with him after tea. Ryan didn't like the sound of that. It meant he was going to be punished. Ryan knew all about punishments, and he wondered what would it would be this time. Perhaps he would be sent to his room. That wasn't a proper punishment at all in his eyes, because he loved spending time there (although if they had thought of removing his TV or laptop from his room he mightn't have been so happy!)

Ryan wondered if they might decide to cancel the Cantadora's visit as a punishment. She was coming to see him for the first time the following night, and he was looking forward to it. (You'll hear more about the Cantadora as the story unfolds, but for the moment let's just say she is an old lady who sometimes comes to visit what are commonly known as 'troubled children')

When the three of them sat down around the kitchen table together, Mum began talking in a serious voice. Mum was a tiny lady, slim and neat like a Barbie doll, and not scary looking in the slightest. Yet there was something about her that always made Ryan nervous when he was in trouble. He tried doing some Tooth Tapping, but somehow with Mum it didn't work very well.

'Ryan, you've had more than enough chances. You need to realise now - if things don't improve, you are going to be suspended'

Ryan looked up, suspicious.

'What do you mean?' he asked.

'I mean you won't be allowed into school for a few days'

'Really?' asked Ryan. He could hardly believe his ears. This was fantastic.

'Yes, really. And if it happens for a second time, you could be suspended for longer'

'Really?' he asked again.

The look of delight on Ryan's face might have seemed obvious to you or me, but Mum took it to be a look of amazement, and she was pleased. 'Maybe for once I'm getting through to him!' she thought.

'Yes, I'm perfectly serious. And in the end you could even be expelled….Meaning, in case you don't fully understand, that you would be put right out of the school - permanently!'

Ryan said nothing. But he was very puzzled. He had expected a punishment and instead it seemed he could be leaving school and never going back. Nothing could have pleased him more!

'Well, have you anything to say for yourself?'

Ryan was almost afraid to speak, in case she changed her mind. He decided to change the subject.

'Is the Cantadora coming to see me tomorrow?'

'Yes, she is. We thought about cancelling her, but it would have been rude at such short notice. And anyway we're hoping she'll help you mend your ways'

The idea of not having to go to school sounded like a dream come true to Ryan. He went back to his room, but was too excited even to go on with his List Making. This

13

could be the end of all his problems, he thought. Danny and he might stop hating each other if they didn't have to go to school together. Danny might even become the friend he had always longed for!

It felt like one of the happiest moments of his life. He ran to Danny's room to tell him.

Danny got up from his Play Station and wedged the bottom of the door with his foot, to stop Ryan from opening it too wide.

'Well, freak? What did Mum and Dad do to you?' he asked.

'I might be suspended' he boasted. 'Even expelled!'

'And that's a good thing?' sneered Danny.

'Yeah. It means I won't have to go to school any more'

Danny burst out laughing.

'You're such a moron, Ryan. Of course you will. If you get expelled, they'll just send you away to Freak School'

Ryan's face fell.

'That's not true. Maria says I'm not a freak'

'You are'

'I'm not'

'Freak! Freak! Freak!' taunted Danny. 'All children have to go to *some* school. You didn't think they'd let you sit at home writing your stupid lists, did you?'

Ryan's heart sank. He knew what Danny was saying made sense. And for the first time in ages, tears began to well up in his eyes. Now I have to tell you, Ryan was not a boy who cried very often - but then it's not every day he had a dream snatched away like that.

Danny ignored his tears.

'Now get out of my room before I *kill* you'

'You don't really mean that'

'I DO! Now leave'

'But Maria said…'

'Maria doesn't know what she is talking about. I *will* kill you'

'You won't'

'Just watch me. I'll sneak up on you - some time when you're least expecting it'

At last Ryan's temper began to crack.

'What if I kill you first?'

'Yeah, yeah!' taunted Ryan. 'You and whose army?'

'I don't need an army. I'll kill you with my bare hands' threatened Ryan.

He had started to push against Danny's door with his full weight.

'You haven't a hope, mate' said Danny, as the two of them began to scuffle in the doorway.

And within moments, a full-scale fight had broken out between the boys, with yelling and shoving and thumping and kicking going on all directions.

Fights between Ryan and Danny were never very fair. Because even though Ryan was extremely agile and fantastic at climbing, he was tiny for his age and very light, so he always ended up coming off worst.

When the rest of the family heard the commotion, they came running upstairs. Dad managed to break it up, but not before a considerable amount of damage was done in the hall and bedroom.

'Ryan started it, Dad' said Danny. 'I was only protecting myself'

'But did you wind him up as usual?' asked Dad crossly. For if there was one thing Dad hated it was for Danny to 'wind Ryan up'

'No way!' lied Danny. 'He came to my room looking for trouble. He tried to kick the door down. He was like a madman!'

At this point Ryan was too upset to speak. For there were two things in the world that he hated with all his heart – one was lying; the other was being blamed in the wrong.

'Danny's a liar' he thought to himself. 'I was not *looking* for trouble. As usual I managed to find it without even looking'

As he stumbled back to his room in tears, he kicked out viciously at everything in his path.

Mum buried her face in her hands.

'I don't know what we're going to do with him' she said.

They decided to leave him on his own for a while to calm down, and then Dad went and spoke to him again.

'Ryan, son' he said gently, 'you really *must* sort yourself out. If you don't, you know the school could throw you out on your ear'

As Ryan looked up, Dad noticed fear in his son's eyes as well as tearstains on his cheeks. Sitting down next to him, he felt tears well up in own eyes as well.

'Cheer up, son' he said gently. 'Maybe the Cantadora will be able to help you'

Chapter 3

MEETING THE
CANTADORA

Ryan hardly slept a wink that night. Without realising it, Dad had given him yet another thing to worry about. When he said the school might *'throw him out on his ear'* a picture had formed in Ryan's head, where he was flung to the ground and landed on his ear. Ouch! Even the thought was painful.

He had so many things to worry about now. Being sent to Freak School was one of them. By now he'd worked out that Freak School must be the *'it'* Mum was talking about that time when she said he was *'really going to get it'*. And even though he had no idea what Freak School was, he knew it must be something dreadful, and the idea of ending up there frightened the life out of him.

With a sigh he reached far under his mattress and pulled out a bright red notebook that Dad had given him the other day. He liked it, and had decided to keep it as a Secret Journal. But so far he hadn't written anything in it, except the words 'Important Lists-PRIVATE' across the front.

Opening the very first page, he decided to start a new and very private list. Here's what he wrote:

List of Serious Worries pertaining to myself, Ryan Gillespie
1) *Being sent to Freak School*
2) *Serious ear injury (from being thrown out of school on my ear, like Dad said)*

Actually, Ryan thought, the worst thing of all was having a murderer for a brother! Granted, he hadn't committed any murders yet, but to Ryan it was only a matter of time. He had hardly slept a wink the night before, in case Danny might creep in to his room and kill him, just as he had threatened.

So he added a third worry to his private list:

3) *Being murdered by my twin brother, Danny Gillespie*

He pictured the other children in school going into convulsions of laughter when they found out he had been murdered by his twin brother. So after some deliberation he added a fourth:

4) *Danny having all the friends at school and me having none*

It's really such a pity that Ryan never thought of sharing his secret worries with anyone, for if he had, I'm sure things would have worked out very differently. But unfortunately he was a boy who kept his worries to himself. At times he could be very chatty, but whenever he was anxious he always went very quiet, and nobody could tell what was going on in his head.

He read over the list with a sigh. There must be *something* he could do - but what? Ryan hadn't a clue where to start.

One thing was clear to him at least. He needed to stay out of trouble at school. Maybe what Maria said was a good idea - that he should make some friends of his own. What Maria didn't realise, though, was that Ryan had absolutely no idea how. He had never taken much interest in other children, and most of the time their games confused or bored him.

However a few times the next day he sidled up close to groups of children and raised his hand in the same way he did when he wanted to speak to the teacher. Ryan had never noticed that children don't do this to other children. But the other children didn't notice him anyway, hanging around the edge of their little groups, so after a while he wandered off his own.

At least one thing was making him happy at the moment. He was looking forward to the evening, when he would meet the Cantadora for the first time.

Mum was pleased that Ryan agreed to even *see* the Cantadora. She had taken him to see so many doctors and 'experts' during his life - at some considerable trouble and expense, I might add! But none of them had made the slightest difference - No one seemed to know what was 'wrong' with Ryan, or how to help him, or how he could be made to behave properly. So by this stage Mum had more or less given up on experts.

But the Cantadora was different. A lady in the library had recommended her to Mum, and Mum decided to mention it to Ryan, just in case. Mum liked the sound of her when she heard that she didn't charge any money. And Ryan liked the sound of her because in his mind it was such a beautiful word. 'Cantadora' he repeated to himself, intrigued.

At eight o'clock exactly, the bell rang and Mum opened the front door to reveal the Cantadora. Ryan smiled with delight the moment he saw her - because she looked *exactly* how he had imagined. A white-haired old lady, with a round crinkly sort of face and a slightly crooked hat. She reached out her hand to greet Mum and Ryan in turn, and as she introduced herself, Ryan noticed she had a slow – you could even say a slightly drawly, voice.

Mum led the way into the front room and chatted politely while Ryan looked on.

'Thanks for coming to see us' Mum said, showing her to a seat, 'though I'm not sure I actually got your name'

'It's OK' said the Cantadora with a twinkle in her eye. 'You know I'm 'The Cantadora', of course. But if you like you can call me Cantadora for short'

Ryan laughed out loud - she has my type of humour, he thought! The Cantadora looked over at him and smiled.

Mum seemed a bit uneasy.

'Em....' she said, 'Miss Watson in the library said you don't charge any fee. But honestly, I would be happier if we had some kind of payment arrangement'

'There's no payment needed' said Cantadora.

'Are you sure?'

'Absolutely!' she said. 'If I can help Ryan, *that* will be my payment'

Mum stayed in the room chatting to her for a while, before leaving the two of them to get to know each other.

From the very start Ryan liked the Cantadora. Better

still, the Cantadora seemed to really like him! And before the evening was over, Ryan flew up to his room and brought down a selection of his lists to show her. The Cantadora read them with great interest, asking questions about every single one. Then she started rummaging in her straw shopping bag.

'It looks like the gift I brought for you will come in *very* useful' she said, handing him a little box.

Ryan was delighted when he opened it. It was a gold Parker pen! He inspected it with pride and noticed it had his name engraved on it in curly italic lettering.

Ryan Jeremy Gillespie

'I've never had a pen with my name on it before' he said, impressed.

'You can use it for your List Making' she replied.

Ryan was thrilled when she said that. The Cantadora obviously thought his List Making was very important - unlike Danny who always said it was weird. (Mum and Dad never actually called it weird, but when they noticed him spending hours on it, they tried to get him to do something else more useful instead)

'Thanks, Cantadora!' he said, trying it out.

'Don't lose it now!' she warned.

'No way!' he replied with conviction.

'Why are you called the Cantadora anyway?' he asked her after a bit.

'Cantadora is an ancient word' she told him. 'It means 'Story Keeper"

'Story Keeper?' said Ryan. 'So do you tell stories

then?'

'Sometimes. Though my job is really a kind of Treasure Hunter'

That sounded more interesting!

'Treasure Hunter?' he repeated. 'What kind of treasure?'

'You see, Ryan, every story contains a hidden message. And in the best stories the message is so valuable it's actually a treasure'

'Really?' said Ryan, surprised.

'Yes. But, like many treasures, it can remain completely hidden till we look for it'

'I don't like stories' said Ryan bluntly.

'You don't?'

'No. I don't read storybooks. Only factual ones'

The Cantadora laughed.

'Did you *ever* enjoy stories?'

Ryan cast his mind back and remembered story time at nursery. It was a happy memory. Even though he always insisted on sitting at the very edge, at a distance from the other children, he usually became absorbed in the story, and in the sound of the teacher's voice.

He told the Cantadora what he had remembered.

'Good' she said. 'Now, I'd like you to do something for me'

'What?'

'First of all, close your eyes for a moment'

Ryan closed his eyes, as she had asked.

'Now, before you have time to think - about anything at all - I want you to tell me the very first story that comes in to your mind'

'The Ugly Duckling' Ryan replied, after only a split

second's hesitation.

'Wonderful!' she exclaimed. 'Now open your eyes'

'How's it wonderful?'

'We will do our Treasure Hunting in the "The Ugly Duckling" story'

Ryan wished he had thought of something better.

'But that's a babyish story' he protested.

'Not at all!' the Cantadora protested. 'The Ugly Duckling is a timeless classic'

'I didn't know that' said Ryan, surprised.

'We'll see how much of it we can remember between us' said the Cantadora. 'Let's see now, how does it start?'

And she settled down and started the story.

'It was the end of summer' she began. *'And down by the river a Mother Duck was brooding on her nest of eggs. At last the eggs began to tremble and shake, and little cracks appeared. One by one the eggs hatched. The Mother Duck admired her new ducklings as they staggered and peeped. Only one egg still remained....'*

'Oh yeah, I remember' interrupted Ryan. 'That was the ugly egg, wasn't it?'

'It was certainly a lot bigger than the other eggs' she answered. 'But you're right - when it eventually hatched, it was big and ugly'

'With pink eyes!' added Ryan

'That's right' laughed the Cantadora.

'It got bullied too, didn't it, Cantadora? And laughed at?'

'Indeed! The Mother Duck tried her best to protect it, but the Ugly Duckling had a hard time. He could find no place where he was happy and at home......'

This is just a babyish story, Ryan admitted to himself. He had put up with enough teasing over the years to let him know it was not cool to be interested in 'babyish' things. But Ryan enjoyed listening to the Cantadora's story anyway. He was, as Mum and Dad often said 'a very odd mixture' of a boy. Sometimes Ryan seemed like he was so much older and wiser than his years. And other times, like when he was with the Cantadora that evening, he seemed a lot younger.

All of a sudden the Cantadora stopped and looked at her watch.

'Good gracious! Is that the time?' she said, getting up to leave.

'But what happened next, Cantadora?'

'We can talk about it next time we meet. In the mean time you have a think, and see what you can remember'

'But what about the hidden message? When will we find it?'

'Patience, Ryan!' she said, smiling 'Treasure hunting should never be rushed'.

Chapter 4

RYAN'S MASTERPLAN

It was lunchtime at school. Ryan was glad it was raining because it meant the class had to stay indoors - and he had an important job to do. Reaching into the pocket of his jacket, he pulled out his Secret Journal. The reason he had brought it into school was that it contained something he had prepared the night before, using his 'Cantadora Pen' as he liked to call it. As you might guess, it was one of his lists. But this was a very important list. In fact it was so important he called it his 'Masterplan'!

Here's what it said:

Ryan Jeremy Gillespie – My Masterplan
List of things I must do in order to make sure I
*   don't:*
*   a. Get thrown out on my ear, or*
*   b. Get sent away to Freak School*
*   1.   Toe the line*
*   2.   Make at least one friend.*

He couldn't think of any others, so he had stopped there. But below this he had written

Class List :
*   Possible friends in alphabetical order:*

There followed an accurate list of every pupil in the class. Ryan remembered this perfectly from daily registration.

'Which one is *Anderson, Peter*?' he asked Kev. (Kev, as you might remember, was the boy who sat next to him)

'That guy over there' said Kev. 'Why?'

Ryan didn't answer, but Kev watched him walk over to Peter Anderson and tap him on the shoulder. Peter turned round from the group he was talking to, and Ryan said something to him. Kev couldn't hear what Ryan had said, but Peter obviously found it amusing.

'No way!' he laughed, turning back to his group.

When Ryan came back to his desk, he consulted his Class List and carefully ruled a line through Peter Anderson's name using his Cantadora Pen.

'Which one is *Bennett, Michael*?' he asked Kev next.

'The ginger guy right next to Peter Anderson. Why do you want to know? What are you up to, Ryan?'

But Ryan just stuffed his Secret Journal in his pocket and approached Michael Bennett, the same way as he'd approached Peter Anderson - only to get the same response. Soon the whole group was laughing and they headed over to where Danny was sitting, to tell him what was going on.

Ryan repeated this strange ritual a few more times with other people from his Class List, until it seemed most of the class was laughing at him. But still he wouldn't tell Kev what was going on, so that in the end Kev had to investigate for himself.

'Ryan!' he hissed, snatching the Secret Journal out of his hand. 'You can't just go round ordering people to be your friend. That's stupid'

'Why's it stupid?' said Ryan, grabbing it back.

'Well for a start, Danny knows what you are up to now, and there's no way he'll *let* anyone in the class be your friend'

'Are you sure?'

'Yeah. Everyone in the class likes Danny. No one will want to get on the wrong side of him'

'No one?'

'No one.....Unless you count Ivan Kelly! He's about the only one who wouldn't care what Danny thought'

'Ivan Kelly will have to be my friend then' Ryan said, decidedly.

'No, Ryan!' said Kev sternly. 'I'm only kidding. Ivan Kelly would eat you up for breakfast!'

Ryan was puzzled.

'Why? Is he a cannibal?'

'Listen, I'm serious! You keep well away from Ivan Kelly'

Ryan looked disappointed.

'Look, I'll be your friend if you like' offered Kev after a while. 'I don't mind falling out with Danny'

Ryan didn't seem keen at first.

'What's your surname then?' he asked, poring over his Class List.

'That's me there' said Kev, pointing '*Shepherd, Kevin*'

'Well, OK' said Ryan begrudgingly.

'So why did you not just ask me in the first place?'

Ryan looked at his alphabetical list.

'I hadn't got to the S's yet' he explained.

'Thanks a lot, mate!' laughed Ken. 'And by the way, if we're going to stay friends, you'll have to stop ignoring me from now on'

'Oh, OK' said Ryan.

Later that day, he wrote in his red book:

Masterplan - Progress Report

> *Made 1 new friend - Kev (nb – proper name Kevin, not Kev) Shepherd*

And in case he would forget, below that he wrote:

Reminder
> *In order to stay friends with Kevin, don't ignore him any more.*

So Ryan had a friend now. That was real progress! From then on he kept his Secret Journal and his Cantadora Pen hidden under his mattress when he was at home. And whenever he went out, he put them into his pocket and carried them with him, in case any more ideas came to him.

And he was doing his best to 'toe the line' as well. Kev was turning out to be a great help to him here, because he told Ryan exactly what the teacher expected from him. Before long even Miss Neill said she noticed a 'marked improvement'. Maybe he wouldn't have to go to Freak School or end up 'out on his ear' after all. He certainly hoped so.

But he couldn't relax yet. How could he? He had one very big worry. And I bet you'd be worried too if you thought you were sharing a home with a murderer who was waiting his chance to sneak up and finish you off!

Ryan couldn't get Danny's threat out of his head. And worst of all, he was on his own in this one. Not one single person in the whole family took his fears seriously. Mum actually *laughed* when he told her.

'Lighten up, Ryan. All brothers fight'

'Lighten up!' he thought angrily. 'What's the use of lightening up when you could be killed at any moment?'

And when Ryan said he needed security cameras in his bedroom his parents had laughed so hard that Ryan stormed off to his room and banged the door. Sometimes adults could be so stupid!

Since his family had refused to do anything to protect him, Ryan realised he would have to think of a way to protect himself. So he decided to expand his Masterplan. Here is what he came up with:

~~~~~~

Ryan's Masterplan, continued:

List of ideas to prevent the murder of myself, Ryan Gillespie
1) *Kill Danny first (very major problem – Murder is A. illegal and B. wrong)*
2) *Keep my bedroom locked at all times*

~~~~~~

Unfortunately Idea Number 2 idea didn't work very well because he had no lock on his bedroom door and Mum refused to get him one. So he had to resort to pushing his wardrobe across his door to block it. In the end Mum got really cross one morning when he slept in and was late for school -Nobody could get his door open!

Ryan managed to sleep like a baby while the rest of the family tried to waken him by yelling at the tops of their voices, and even bashing pots and pans together to make a racket!

'This is ridiculous, Ryan' Mum said when he eventually emerged. 'We are not having locked doors and barricaded rooms in this house. What if there was a fire?'

Ryan didn't know how a fire was any more serious than a murder, but he was getting used to how stupid adults can be.

He tried sleeping with one eye open but of course that was impossible. So he developed a strange way of lying in bed at night. He would lie on his side facing the door, with one arm held out in front of him and one behind, ready to face attack if necessary. It was very uncomfortable but it was the best he could come up with.

In the end his brainwave came to him completely by accident!

You see, ever since he and Kev had talked about Ivan Kelly, Ryan hadn't been able get the conversation out of his head. He remembered exactly what Kev had said about Ivan, word for word.

'He would eat you up for breakfast'

This really bothered Ryan. Was Ivan Kelly a cannibal or was he not? If so, then surely the authorities should be informed.

He decided to ask Kev about it one day.

'Kevin' he asked. 'Is Ivan Kelly a cannibal?'

Kev was getting used to Ryan's strange ideas by now.

'No' he replied. 'But you better keep out of his way

all the same'

'Why?'

'Look, Ryan, Ivan Kelly is just trouble' Kev whispered. 'The whole Kelly family are in and out of prison so much they're known locally as "The Kelly Gang". I've heard my Grandfather talking about them. He says they're a bad lot'

'Why are they called "The Kelly Gang"?'

''Cos they're a bunch of gangsters, I suppose' said Kev, giggling.

'Seriously?'

'Yeah. I reckon that's why nobody would get on the wrong side of Ivan'

'What do you mean?'

'It would be like taking on the whole Kelly Gang – you'd probably end up dead or something!'

That evening while he was trying to get to sleep, Ryan played back the conversation in his head. Ivan Gillespie was so lucky to be a gangster, he thought. Ryan loved watching films about exciting things like gangsters and secret agents. He wished he could be a gangster in real life, just like Ivan. Then he would be safe from Danny!

A new thought began to form in his head.

'If I became a member of The Kelly Gang' he figured, 'Danny would be too scared to attack or kill me'

He reached under his mattress to where he had hidden his Secret Journal. Then turning to his Master Plan, he added his new thought at the bottom of the page under his '*List of ideas to prevent the murder of myself, Ryan Gillespie*'

'*Idea No. 3*' he wrote with satisfaction - '*Join The Kelly Gang*'

Chapter 5

JOINING THE KELLY GANG

In Ryan's mind now, joining the Kelly Gang was his only hope. How else could he protect himself from Danny's murderous threats? The only problem was that he didn't know how to go about joining up! He didn't want to get things wrong again, like the day when he had tried ordering people from his Class List to be his friend. Kev had explained that one to him.

'You can't just *order* people to be your friend, Ryan' he had said. 'You have to be nice to them'

It probably worked the same way for joining a gang, Ryan thought. That night, as he lay awake, he wondered how he could be nice to Ivan Kelly.

But by the following morning he had it all worked out - Joining a gang couldn't possibly have the same rules as making friends. It was obvious -there must be a membership fee!

He went to his money box to see what he could afford. Unfortunately he didn't have much cash at the time. But there was a total of £18.40. Not bad, he thought and stuffed it into his pocket.

Throughout the morning in school, Ryan watched Ivan Kelly carefully. He was a good-looking boy with dark curly hair, and at first Ryan could see nothing unusual about him. But then he observed how rarely Ivan smiled or even looked in anyone else's direction. Kev was right, he noticed with relief. Even the teachers seemed to keep their distance!

Lunchtime would be a good time to talk to him, Ryan thought, especially as it was another horrible day. Not only was it pouring with rain but it was also very cold, meaning the class stayed indoors again for lunch.

Ivan was sitting near the window with his feet up on his desk, reading a magazine. It was probably one of those magazines that the teacher wouldn't have approved of, but if so, she pretended she hadn't noticed. Ryan sidled over and sat next to him.

'Excuse me' he said. (He had decided in advance to be as polite as possible)

Ivan barely glanced up.

'How much does it cost to join the Kelly Gang?'

Ivan went on reading.

'Excuse me' Ryan said again, and repeated his question.

Again Ivan ignored him.

Ryan wasn't sure whether he hadn't heard or whether he hadn't understood. So he decided to try again.

'I would like to join the Kelly Gang' he explained patiently. 'I'm prepared to pay the usual membership fee of course, if you will tell me how much it is. I can afford to pay up to £18.40….. Is that enough?'

Ivan looked up at last.

'Clear off, freak!' he said and went back to his reading.

Ryan wasn't sure what to do now. This hadn't gone according to plan. He supposed he'd just have to try again tomorrow.

That evening the Cantadora came to see him again. She had brought some playing cards with her, and the two of them had fun together as she taught him some new games. Then Ryan asked if they could continue the story of the Ugly Duckling.

'Where had we got to?' asked the Cantadora.

'The Ugly Duckling was being bullied' Ryan volunteered.

And so they went on with the story. The Cantadora told him all about the adventures of the Ugly Duckling as he grew up among the marshes - how the other ducks hissed and screeched at him no matter where he went.

'They laughed at him too, didn't they?' said Ryan.

'Oh, yes'

'Why did they laugh at him?

'Because he was different to them'

'That's stupid'

'Are you ever laughed at, Ryan?'

'Suppose so' he answered, quietly.

At that a silence fell between them for a while.

'What else can you remember of the story?' asked the Cantadora eventually.

'Nothing' said Ryan sullenly.

'Never mind' she said brightly. 'We'll leave it there for the meantime'

A bit later Ryan asked her a question, which had been on his mind.

'Cantadora' he said. 'Do you think I will ever be stronger than my brother?'

'An interesting question!' replied the Cantadora.

'However you'll have to find the answer for yourself'

'How?'

'Let me tell you a little story which might help you' she said. 'It's called "The Sun and the Wind"'

> *'One day the sun and the wind were arguing about which one of them was stronger.*
>
> *The wind was boasting – "I am stronger than you. I can even blow down a mighty oak tree"*
>
> *"Let's have a competition to settle it' said the sun. And he pointed to a man walking along a country path "See that man down there. Let's see which of us can get the coat off his back"*
>
> *The wind tried first. He blew harder and harder till there was quite a gale. But the harder he blew, the tighter the man pulled his coat around him and in the end he gave up.*
>
> *Then the sun had a turn. He shone warmly and steadily till at last the man became too hot and removed his coat"*

'What's story of The Sun and The Wind got to do with Danny and me?' asked Ryan, puzzled

'Think about the story's hidden message. It will help you find the answer to your question'

'But what is its hidden message?'

'Perhaps that you can be powerful, like the sun, without being forceful and mean'

'Is that really true?' asked Ryan.

'I'll tell you what. You have a think about it' she said. 'You'll need to make your own mind'

Ryan did have a think about it. It was a nice story, he thought, but its message was silly. Being gentle and kind like the sun would never make him powerful enough - Not when his own twin brother had threatened his life. So he decided to have another go at joining the Kelly Gang.

The next day, he remembered to bring his £18.40 to school, but he forgot his Secret Journal. However he managed to find a loose sheet on which to do some more work on his Masterplan, intending to copy it in to his Secret Journal later. Here's what he wrote:

Masterplan —Progress Report.
I still need to join the Kelly Gang

Problem – Ivan will not tell me how much membership
*   fee is.*
I don't know who else I could ask.

Ideas List
Idea 1 – Ask Ivan again
*   (nb Be polite)*
Idea 2 – Is there another gang I could join instead?
Idea 3 – Offer Ivan the full £18.40

(Problem – what is it's not enough?)

(It's unfortunate that as usual Ryan never thought of telling anyone what was on his mind. And also that he chose moments to talk to Ivan when Kev wasn't about, because otherwise things could have worked out very differently)

In the end he decided on Idea 3. He took his money out of his pocket and sidled over to Ivan again. Ivan continued reading and didn't look up.

'I've got my membership fee' he boasted. 'Look - £18.40'

Then when Ivan kept ignoring him, 'You can have the lot!' he said, holding the money in front of Ivan's nose.

Ivan reached out a large muscular hand and grabbed Ryan round the wrist. Slowly he began squeeze, harder and harder.

'That's sore!' complained Ryan. But Ivan just peeled back Ryan's fingers till the money dropped onto his desk. Then, without a word, he picked it up, put it in his pocket and walked out of the room.

Ryan didn't like having his wrist crushed of course. But on the bright side he supposed he must be a member of the Kelly Gang now, given the fact that his membership fee had been accepted. But just to be sure, he thought he'd better check it out with Ivan after school. So as soon as the bell rang, Ryan headed after him as he rushed out of the school gates.

Ivan was walking so quickly that he didn't even notice he was being followed. He had his head down and his shoulders hunched up against the stormy wind. Half way down Downshire Road, he dodged into an alleyway and joined a stocky looking man with dark hair and a moustache. The man was Nick Kelly, Ivan's cousin. He had just been released from prison where he had served a lengthy term for a string of offences.

Ryan didn't know this of course, as he approached the two of them.

Chapter 6

NICK KELLY

'Who's this then?' asked Nick Kelly.

Ivan was embarrassed when he realised Ryan had followed him.

'Sorry, Nick. I told him to clear off earlier' he said.

Nick seemed intrigued.

'What do you want, kiddo?' he asked.

'I'm a new member of the Kelly Gang' said Ryan proudly.

'Wise up' said Ivan.

'Well, if I'm not, I demand a refund!' said Ryan indignantly, 'for I have paid my membership fee in full.'

'Have you indeed?' asked Nick with amusement. 'How much did you pay?'

'£18.40!' Ryan answered. 'And I paid it because I want to be a real life gangster!'

He was getting quite worked up now. If there was one thing he hated, it was unfairness. So he assumed his most haughty tone:

'If I'm not a member' he protested, 'then money has been taken from me under false pretences!'

But Ivan and Nick just laughed at him, which made Ryan even more upset.

'This is no laughing matter!' he yelled. 'I have my mobile phone with me, and I will report this matter to the highest authorities'

To prove his point Ryan reached into his pocket and pulled out his mobile phone. Unfortunately, in doing so he accidentally pulled out the *Masterplan* that he had been working on as well; and before he could grab it and put it back in his pocket, a strong gust of wind swept it along the alleyway and high into the air.

At this point, Ivan and Nick were about to witness yet another unusual thing about Ryan, which was his amazing ability to run and climb. When he was a toddler, his family used to call him 'Monkey Boy'. He nearly drove Mum mad with all his climbing – especially when he used to climb out of the window at night! And if you had seen Ryan that afternoon you would understand how he earned his nickname. He took off after that sheet of paper as if his very life depended on it. (In his eyes it did, don't forget!)

Just as he reached it, another gust blew it beyond his grasp - then another, then another. For several minutes, in pursuit of his *Masterplan,* Ryan ran and climbed over walls, railings and fences, only to have it repeatedly snatched from him his reach at the last moment. The wind in the alleyway seemed to be going round in circles!

At last he saw it fly over a high fence into the back garden of a house next to the alleyway.

Without pausing for a moment, Ryan ran at the wall. Nick and Ivan watched in amazement, as somehow he found footholds and scaled it with ease. Then, jumping down into the garden, he at last retrieved his *Masterplan* and stuffed it back in his pocket.

Ivan and Nick were staring in amazement.

'You know how to climb!' observed Nick, as he ran back towards them.

'I know' said Ryan in a matter-of-fact tone. 'I'm an

excellent climber'

But it was gang membership that he wanted to talk about - not climbing.

'Well' he demanded, 'am I getting a refund or am I a member of the Kelly Gang? '

'You're in!' said Nick, reaching out to shake hands with him.

'NICK!' said Ivan. 'Stop messing around'

But Nick ignored him and addressed Ryan instead.

'You know, kiddo, you're dead right' he said. 'Of course you're a member. You've paid your dues, fair and square'

'What are you even talking to a freak like him for?' Ivan asked, tugging his cousin's sleeve.

'Did you see how he can climb? It's amazing'

'Listen, Nick, he's a real freak!' protested Ivan. 'I mean proper weird. Not right in the head, you know'

'I'm *not* a real freak!' yelled Ryan angrily.

'Course you're not' said Nick in a mock gentle voice. 'You're a real, paid up *gangster!*'

Shortly after that, he told Ryan to run off home.

Ryan did so happily. The day was turning out well after all, he decided. He had accomplished what he'd set out to do - He had joined the Kelly Gang! Nick even said he was a *'real gangster'.* Ryan liked that title. It sounded very important – a bit like a famous movie character. Surely now he would be safe from Danny, his murderous brother!

Just as he ran along Belmont Road, two elderly gentlemen stepped out of No.49. It looked like they were going for a walk. A gust of wind immediately swept the hat right off the head of one of them. And for the second time that day, Ryan was reminded of the story of the sun and the wind.

'The sun wouldn't have been strong enough to do *that*!' he thought with conviction.

Then, with as much skill and flourish as he had used to retrieve his *Masterplan*, he chased the hat as it flew up trees and over garden walls. The two men stood and watched in amazement, exactly as Ivan and Nick had done.

'Look at that kid climb!' said one of them. 'He's like a monkey in the zoo'

'Very good of him, all the same' laughed the other. 'Going to all that trouble for an old man's hat!'

Eventually Ryan handed it back to its owner.

'Thanks very much!' began the old man.

But Ryan had run on already.

'Here, son' he called after him, 'what's your name?'

But Ryan was out of earshot already. He could hardly wait to get home and tell Danny his news.

'I've joined the Kelly Gang' he boasted as he flew in the door.

Danny burst out laughing.

'Seriously. I'm a real gangster now'

'Very funny, Ryan'

'It's not funny'

'Yeah, just imagine you being in the Kelly Gang'

'I don't have to imagine. It's true'

'And you expect me to believe that?'

'Yes. So you better treat me right or else you'll have the whole Kelly Gang after you!'

'You're such a liar, Ryan'

Ryan sighed with frustration. Why wouldn't Danny believe him?

He decided not to mention the business of the Kelly Gang to anyone else until he talked to Ivan again. Surely he should have been given a membership card or something in order to *prove* that he was a real gangster. He had paid his membership fee after all!

That evening the Cantadora came, which took his mind off the Kelly Gang. After they played cards for a while, he asked her to go on with the Ugly Duckling story, because he still couldn't remember how it turned out. But the Cantadora said no, that tonight they were going to have 'a time of reflection'

'You see' she explained, 'stories are like mirrors'

'How are they like mirrors?' asked Ryan, looking unconvinced.

'If we learn how to look into them, we can see parts of parts of ourselves reflected back'

Ryan was puzzled.

Then the Cantadora asked him what parts of himself he saw reflected in the story of the Ugly Duckling.

'None' he said without hesitation.

'None at all?'

'Of course not!' he said indignantly. 'I'm not a duck. I don't look anything like a duck - Or any other kind of farmyard animal!'

'No, no' smiled the Cantadora, 'In order to find the hidden message, you must think about what the characters are like on the *inside*. Forget about outside appearances…. Are there any of them you feel strongly about?'

'No'

'What about the Ugly Duckling. How do you feel about him?'

Ryan shrugged.

'He's OK'

'Well, is there anyone you *don't* like then?' she persisted.

'Yeah, I hate all those other ducks – you know, the ones who laugh at the Ugly Duckling'

'Good for you! Hatred's a strong feeling. What do you hate about them?'

'They're mean'

'What do they do that is mean?'

'They laugh at the Ugly Duckling'

'And laughing at other people is mean?'

'Yeah!'

'How do you know, Ryan?'

'Because I know kids who laugh at other kids'

'Do they laugh at you?'

'Sometimes' he muttered.

'Why do they laugh at you?

'Dunno'

'Are you a bit different to the other children perhaps, in the same way the Ugly Duckling is different to other ducklings?'

'No' said Ryan, sounding angry. 'I look completely normal. There are even two people in my class who are smaller than me and they have plenty of friends!'

'I told you, forget about outside appearances! What about on the inside?'

'Oh, I forgot' said Ryan.

He thought for a moment.

'I suppose I think differently to other children' he admitted.

'And do you ever behave differently?'

'Sometimes'

'So how does you feel when you're laughed at?'

'I *hate* it!'

'So you see —the story has mirrored a part of you'

But just at that point, when Ryan was getting interested, she decided it was time to stop - as she all too often seemed to do!

'We can talk more next time' she said, gathering up her belongings.

'But when will we find the hidden message?' asked Ryan

'Remember what I told you, Ryan. Treasure Hunting is not to be rushed. You need to take time to think things over'

To give Ryan his due, he did think about it. He saw now that the Ugly Duckling reflected the part of him that hated to feel different and lonely and laughed at. But that didn't take him any closer to finding the story's hidden message! So he thought about his Gang Membership Card instead. He wanted to ask Ivan about it, but Ivan didn't show up at school the next day.

That afternoon as he walked home on his own, he decided to go via the alleyway at Downshire Road again, in the hope of spotting Ivan. What Ryan didn't know was that there was someone hanging around the area, who was just as anxious to find him, as he was to find Ivan.

As he walked along, he suddenly heard a voice calling

after him.

'Hey, kiddo!'

He looked round.

It was Nick Kelly, Ivan's cousin.

Chapter 7

'SECRET AGENTS'

Although Ryan didn't realise it at the time, this meeting would prove to be a real turning point in his young life; because Nick Kelly had just set upon a very sinister path. To put it plainly, he was determined to corrupt young Ryan. And by that I mean he was planning to turn him into a young criminal, if he could. Nick Kelly was quite prepared to lie to Ryan and hurt him any way that suited, if it helped his own criminal plans.

'I've found myself a right little Oliver Twist' he had boasted to Stevie Myers, over a few beers in the local pub.

Stevie Myers was an older man, who had been close to the Kellys for years. Despite that, he managed to stay more or less on the right side of the law, and even ran a small business in the High Street - a 'While U Wait' shop, which cut keys and mended shoes.

'What are you on about, Nick?' Stevie had wanted to know.

'This kid out of Ivan's class. He's perfect' Nick said by way of explanation.

'What do you mean he's perfect?'

'A bit simple in the head, according to Ivan. No friends. Very gullible......And you should see how he can climb!'

'What on earth have you got up your sleeve, Nick?' asked Stevie.

'I'm going to play him along. Tell him he's a Secret

47

Agent or some rubbish - Tell him anything that will keep him happy. Then I'll train him up the Nick Kelly way'

'The Nick Kelly way?' repeated Stevie.

'Exactly!' boasted Nick. 'Before you know it, I'll have turned him into one perfect little cat burglar!'

Ryan knew none of this of course when he met Nick that afternoon after school.

'I was looking for Ivan' he said as Nick approached.

Nick had made sure Ivan stayed away from school that day, because he wanted to get talking to Ryan on his own.

'What for?'

'I need a Gang Membership Card'

'What for?'

'To prove I'm a real member of the Kelly Gang'

'Why's that, kiddo?'

'Otherwise people won't believe I'm really a member'

'Who did you tell?'

'My twin brother'

'And he didn't believe you?'

'No'

'Anyone else?'

'No'

'That's good. You mustn't tell anyone else now, kiddo'

'But it's really important for them to know'

'Why's that then?'

Ryan hesitated before he replied, wondering how much to reveal. It's a real pity that of all the people he could have chosen to confide in, at that moment, that afternoon he chose Nick.

'Nick Kelly could be my only chance of protection from Danny', he thought. In Ryan's mind, after all, his life had been threatened - and Mum and Dad had done nothing to help.

'The thing is' he confided, 'my life is in danger'

'Really?' said Nick, surprised.

'Really!' said Ryan solemnly. 'You see, my brother said he is going to kill me. And all my parents have done about it is to laugh'

'Oh, no!' said Nick in mock horror.

'I figured that if I joined the Kelly Gang, I would be safe. Because no one would dare murder a member of the Kelly Gang'

'Don't worry, kiddo. As long as you're in my gang, you'll be safe. I won't let anyone kill you'

Ryan was relieved to hear that.

'So I really *am* a gangster then?'

'Yeah, of course'

'Will I meet any other gang members soon?'

'Oh, no! I've decided to make you my Secret Agent'

'Wow!' said Ryan, delighted.

'Tell me this, kiddo. Are you good at keeping secrets?'

'Of course'

'Good for you!' said Nick. 'Just as long as you promise to keep everything secret between us, I'll keep you nice and safe'

'I promise' said Ryan, beaming.

And when Nick told him to run along now, he did so happily. Another day had turned out well, he thought. Not only was he a Real Gangster, he was a Secret Agent now too!

Later that evening he wrote proudly in his Secret Journal:

Masterplan Progress Report, continued –
Made 1 more new friend – Nick Kelly.
Also joined the Kelly Gang and became a Secret Agent!

The next time Ryan met the Cantadora she noticed he seemed in good form.

'When will I discover the hidden message?' he asked as soon as she sat down.

'You're getting closer all the time. Tell me, what have you found out for yourself?'

'Well, I can see myself reflected in the Ugly Duckling Story'

'Well done! That's why the story appealed to you when you were small'

'Really?'

'Oh, yes!'

'Wow!'

'And have you been able to remember any more?'

'I remember the bit when the Ugly Duckling saw some swans, but he didn't know what they were'

'Great!' she said. 'We need to start from there then'

And she went on to tell him all about the first time the Ugly Duckling saw swans – the most beautiful creatures he had ever set eyes upon. And how he felt such a deep love in his heart for those great white birds, so far above him. And how the Ugly Duckling struggled alone and miserable throughout the bitter winter.

'Do you ever feel lonely and sad, Ryan?' she asked him.

'Sometimes' he answered.

Just at that moment Ryan felt an urge to tell the Cantadora how much better he was feeling since he'd met Nick Kelly - and how great it was to be a 'Real Gangster' and a 'Secret Agent'. But he knew he couldn't say a word. He couldn't break his promise to Nick.

Being Nick's Secret Agent was fantastic fun for Ryan! From time to time the two of them would arrange to meet in a 'secret meeting place' - usually at the corner of some street or other in Belmont, the area where Ryan lived. Ryan thoroughly enjoyed his time with Nick - he was always happier in the company of an adult than with other children. Especially if that adult gave him one-to-one attention and made him feel important and special, as Nick did.

Nick taught him a game called 'Secret Missions'

'Your Secret Mission is to climb to the top of that tree in sixty seconds' Nick would say.

And of course Ryan scrambled to the top in a flash.

'Fantastic! Your next Secret Mission is to climb over that wall'

'But that's somebody's garden'

'It's OK. They'll never find out'

'Are you sure?'

'You can trust me' said Nick, offering him a square of chocolate.

Before long Mum and Dad noticed that Ryan was coming

in late after school sometimes, or perhaps going out for a walk in the evening.

'I'm very worried about Ryan' Mum said. 'I don't think we should let him go out on his own like that'

'You can't have one rule for Ryan and another for Danny' said Dad.

'But we always know whose house Danny is going to'

'Well, Ryan is different. You know he's a loner'

'But …' began Mum.

'Honestly, Nancy!' said Dad. 'You've nothing to worry about. At least he's getting out. It's better than him sitting in his room all the time like he used to'

'I hope he's not keeping bad company' said Mum. 'I heard him mention somebody called Nick the other day, but Danny says he's never heard of anyone called Nick'

'It's obviously some imaginary friend' Dad reassured her. 'He's probably collecting 'Data' for one of his Lists. More street names or something. I'm sure it's perfectly harmless'

'So you think he's safe OK?'

'Nancy, we can't wrap Ryan in cotton wool all his life' Dad argued. 'I'm sure he'll come to no harm'

One day Ryan got a bit worried about something he heard Kev say. He decided to check it out next time he saw Nick.

'Nick' he said as they walked together one evening. 'The Kelly Gang isn't a *bad* gang, is it?'

'No way!'

'It's just that Kevin Shepherd said the Kelly Gang are a bunch of thugs and criminals'

Nick feigned a look of shock and hurt.

'He just doesn't know us' he said.

'That's true' said Ryan with feeling. 'I mean I know you – and you're a nice person'

'Exactly!'

'And I'm a member of the Kelly Gang and I would never do anything illegal'

'Good for you!' said Nick.

'You don't think climbing into people's gardens is illegal, do you?' he asked anxiously.

'Course not. It's only a game'

Soon the Secret Missions became more and more daring.

'Here's your Secret Mission tonight. You have to climb over that wall, run to the back door of the house, and then back to me. And you must do it without anyone noticing you'

Ryan checked again

'Are you sure it's legal?'

'It's just a game' Ivan reassured him.

'This time your Secret Mission is to check - without anyone noticing you - if the back door is locked' he asked the next time.

'Why?' asked Ryan.

'Just for fun' he answered. Again Ryan did as he was told.

And before long the 'Secret Mission' involved getting inside people's houses without being seen.

A few times Ryan nearly got caught and had to hide for up to half an hour till the coast was clear. And another time a lady turned the water hose on him and yelled nasty names as he made his escape over the fence. But Nick said that was all part of the game, and gave him some chocolate to cheer him up.

At last Nick realised he would never get his Secret Agent to actually steal for him, because in his own way Ryan had a strong sense of right and wrong. So he came up with an even more cunning plan. He would deceive Ryan into 'borrowing' keys for him. That would allow him to make an impression of the keys before getting Ryan to return them. (He had already talked Stevie into making copies of the keys from the impressions – for a hefty fee of course!)

Nick's plan was to use the copy keys at a later time to break in and steal from houses. The more keys he could collect, the more houses he could burgle.

'It's a brainwave!' he boasted to Stevie Myers. 'Ryan can climb over the wall and check the back door - so many people leave them open these days. Then if it's open, he can go in, hunt around, grab a few keys and back out again'

'And what if someone sees him?'

'We'll do it in the evenings. Most people will be sitting in their living room watching TV…. Anyway even if they do see him, they'll just think he's a kid making a nuisance of himself'

'Would you like to play a new game?' he asked Ryan one evening.

'What is it?'

'It's called the Key Game'

'How do you play the Key Game?'

'Have a look around the house and see if you can find

any keys'

'What kind of keys?'

Anything. House keys. Car keys'

'Why?'

'Just think how cool it would be to pinch a key'

'*Pinch* a key?' repeated Ryan, shocked.

'Not *really* pinch of course, kiddo' he said, offering him a piece of chocolate. 'Just borrow. That's how you play the Key Game. You borrow the key and then put the key straight back again, so there's no harm done. Wait till you see. It will be great fun!'

And the first time Ryan played the Key Game, Nick knew he had the breakthrough he wanted. He was quick enough to take an impression of the key while Ryan was looking the other way. And then he made Ryan break back into the house again and put the key back exactly where he found it.

It really hadn't taken long for Nick to do exactly what he set out to do. He had got his 'Secret Agent' involved in dangerous criminal activities.

Chapter 8

EVERYTHING GOES

WRONG

Just for the moment Ryan was happy with life, and he never suspected for a moment that Nick, his new 'friend' was not a friend at all, but an evil, hardened criminal. Because as we know, Ryan was not very good at judging who can be trusted. And, don't forget, Nick Kelly was a very cunning man. He knew exactly how to give Ryan the kind of attention he enjoyed - and lots of chocolate too! So, in Ryan's eyes, Nick was a very kind man.

But before very long Nick had as many keys as he wanted, and had no further need of Ryan, so he decided to end the 'friendship' once and for all. The evening he did so, he took the precaution of deleting his phone number and erasing all messages from Ryan's mobile phone, while pretending to admire it.

In his usual corner of the pub later on, he talked it over with Stevie Myers.

'I'm calling it quits now, Stevie' he said. 'I've enough keys to keep me going'

'What about the kid?'

'Forget him. He's served his purpose'

'Will you get rid of him?' Stevie asked.

'Too dangerous'

'Could he not wreck everything?'

'No. I've been careful'

'Sure?'

'Don't worry. The kid's a bit soft in the head. No one

would listen to him anyway'

Nick concocted a story to tell Ryan, about how he had to go away on business to Pakistan, to explain why he wouldn't be seeing him 'for a while'. Ryan was very disappointed when he heard.

'But I want to be your Secret Agent'

'You're going to be something even more important now. You're going to be an Underground Agent'

'What do you mean?'

'Underground Agents only meet in very secret locations. You see, no one must know that they're part of the gang'

Nick made it sound exciting.

'Like if they meet by accident or something, they might have to pretend they don't know each other' he continued.

'Really?'

'Yes. So as an Underground Agent you'll have to keep our secrets even more carefully till I get back'

'But when will that be?'

'Not sure yet. I'll send you a text in a day or two to let you know' he lied.

And at that, he walked out of Ryan's life as easily as he had walked into it.

Nick Kelly hadn't gone anywhere of course. He was still close by, watching and waiting. And whenever he discovered that someone was away from home, he grabbed his chance. He walked up to the house and let himself in, using the key.

Nick stole only things he could carry in a bag, like cash,

credit cards, jewellery and so on. And he walked in and out of the houses so calmly that no one suspected for an instant that he was up to no good. During the Key Game, he had managed to get a copy cut of every single key that Ryan had handed over to him, which made his task very easy.

Before long the local papers were full of the news, with headlines like these:

> *'Heartache for pensioners as burglaries continue'*
> *'No sign of forced entry -Police baffled'*
> *'Police suspect lone burglar responsible'*

And even though the Police suspected that the culprit was one person operating on his own, they were no nearer to discovering his identity. Local people began to call him 'The Belmont Burglar'.

Ryan took little interest in any of this however. He had other things on his mind, like why Nick still hadn't sent him a text, and how Nick's phone number had suddenly disappeared from his phone so that he couldn't even contact him. Danny hadn't threatened to kill him in a while, but if he was to threaten again, Ryan knew he wouldn't be safe without Nick nearby.

Even if Ryan had read the papers, however, it would never have crossed his mind that the burglaries were anything to do with himself or Nick.

'I've lost someone's number from my phone' he complained urgently at the tea table one evening.

'Whose phone number?' asked Mum.

'A friend'

'That's funny!' said Danny. 'You don't have any

friends'

Dad looked up from behind his newspaper.

'Enough, Danny!' he said in a warning tone.

'I do have friends!' argued Ryan.

'OK then. Name one!'

'Kevin Shepherd' he said triumphantly.

By way of reply, Danny just grunted.

And there was no doubt about it. Ryan and Kev had become friends. However this was mainly due to the fact that Kev felt a bit sorry for Ryan, and was doing his best to make life easier for him. Kev was the kind of boy who shrugged it off when other children teased him by calling him 'Freako's Friend'. He was just glad that things were going a bit better for Ryan. These days Ryan was prepared to actually listen to Kev - even when he was reminding him of what work he was supposed to be doing, or offering a bit of advice to keep him out of trouble!

But then the following day Kev was off school with a tummy upset. And, as you might expect, Miss Neill soon found reason to give off to Ryan again – because without Kev's help, he had little clue what was expected of him.

As you might expect, Danny didn't lose a chance to try and get Ryan into trouble at home.

'Mum, wait till you hear what Ryan said to Miss Neill today' he would begin.

'I don't want to hear this Danny, if you're just telling tales'

'But Ryan said …'

'Look, Danny - was he sent to the headmaster's office or was he not?' she asked.

'No. But he....'

'Well as long as he's kept out of the headmaster's office, then I'm happy. Now be quiet' she snapped. 'If there are any problems that I need to know about, I'm sure the school will let me know'

But Mum was secretly worried about Ryan, as she told Dad later. He was 'far too quiet for her liking' these days.

'Don't worry' Dad reassured her. 'You know he can be very quiet at times'

'No, this is different. He's not even interested in his List Making these days. That's never happened before'

But when she asked Ryan about it, he told her he was leaving his List Making until he found his Cantadora Pen, which had been missing for a while.

In fact, the Cantadora was the only person who could cheer Ryan up these days, when she came to visit. Ryan hadn't been able to remember any more of the Ugly Duckling story, so they'd dropped it for a while, playing cards and chatting about this and that instead. There was something about the Cantadora's matter-of-fact manner that put Ryan at ease. He didn't tell her anything about Nick of course, because that was a secret, but he did tell her about Miss Neill and how he used his 'Tooth Tapping' every time she gave off to him.

And as with just about everything Ryan told her, the Cantadora was most interested when she heard.

'That's a *very* clever idea!' she exclaimed.

'Is it?'

'Of course' she said. 'We all need little tricks to help us deal with people who, as they say, wind us up. I must remember that Tooth Tapping idea myself some time'

It's just a pity Ryan didn't remember it himself the next day in class. If he had, it might have been enough to keep him from ending up in the headmaster's office again.

The problem started when Miss Neill was going round the classroom collecting in the home-works. Ryan was miles away. He was very worried about something he heard earlier. Ryan had decided to approach Ivan at lunchtime.

'I need to contact your cousin Nick urgently' he said.

At first Ivan had ignored him.

'Tell me, when will be back from Pakistan?' persisted Nick.

Ivan burst out laughing at that.

'Pakistan! Is that what he told you? Funny he was in the pub with my brother last night'

This had left Ryan very confused. If Ivan was right, then why had Nick not been in touch with him?

And it was this that he was thinking about and not homework when Miss Neill stopped beside his desk.

'Where's your home-work, Ryan?' she asked.

'Dunno'

'Have you actually done it this time?'

Ryan tried to remember, but he was thinking so hard about Nick that he found it hard to stop thinking about that and start thinking about homework instead. And the harder he tried, the less he could remember.

'I don't know' he muttered eventually.

'In other words "no" ' barked Miss Neill sarcastically, as she marched off.

There was something in her words that caused Ryan's temper to crack without the slightest warning.

'In other words "No"' he repeated to himself silently. He knew what that meant - It meant she didn't believe him! She was accusing him of lying! And as you know, one of the things Ryan hated most was to be blamed in the wrong - Especially of telling lies!

The next words he uttered were shouted in a voice so loud that the entire class seemed to jump.

'I SAID I DON'T KNOW!' he yelled.

Everyone stopped what they were doing, and turned to see what was going on.

'I BEG YOUR PARDON?' asked Miss Neill, turning round.

'You heard me' he yelled. 'You asked if I'd done my homework. I told you "I don't know". I did *not* say "No"'

'Have you *quite* finished, Ryan Gillespie?'

'No! I'm not quite finished. I am not a liar! If I had meant "No" I would have said "No" '

A shocked silence filled the classroom for a few moments, till Miss Neill next spoke.

'How *dare* you address me in that tone?'

'How dare you accuse me of lying?' yelled Ryan.

Naturally Ryan ended up in the headmaster's office, but not before he had got himself into even more trouble by giving a good piece of his mind not only to Miss Neill but also to the 'whole stupid class'.

Mr Stevenson was very disappointed, he said, because he had 'hoped never to see him in his office again'.

Ryan fought back the tears. He had no hope of staying out of Freak School this time.

Chapter 9

ASSAULT ON BELMONT ROAD

Before long, Ryan dearly regretted his outburst in class.

'You've really had it this time' Danny warned him on the way home, with obvious satisfaction.

Ryan didn't answer. He was worrying about Mum's warning. She had said that if he ended up in the headmaster's office again, he was *'really going to get it'*. Now Danny was telling him he'd *'really had it'* - and still Ryan wasn't sure what *'it'* was. What he was really afraid of, though, was that *'it'* was Freak School.

Fortunately Mum and Dad didn't get to hear what had happened that day, because when Danny went to tell them, Mum refused point blank to listen, saying she was 'fed up with Danny carrying tales' But Ryan knew it was only a matter of time till they found out, and the worry of what lay ahead weighed heavily on his mind.

Even the Cantadora noticed a change in his mood that evening. For usually he had plenty to chat to her about, but this time he was very quiet, even with her. The reason for this was not just the trouble in school and his worries about Freak School, but also the fact that he still was missing Nick.

Unfortunately he didn't think of telling this to the Cantadora - or anyone else for that matter.

They played cards quietly for a while.

'Have you remembered any more of the Ugly

Duckling story?' she asked.

'Dunno' sighed Ryan.

'Well then, let's see what we can remember between us'

And that evening they went on to finish the story.

The Cantadora told Ryan how after the long, bitter winter, at last the spring arrived, and the Ugly Duckling grew strong again. And how he stretched his wings and flew high across the land, until he came to a pond where he saw three beautiful swans.

'The Ugly Duckling longed to join the swans' continued the Cantadora, 'but instead he tried to hide from them'

'Why did he try to hide if he longed to be with them?' asked Ryan.

'Perhaps he was ashamed, because he felt so ugly' answered the Cantadora. 'What do you think?'

'Maybe he was afraid they would laugh at him' said Ryan.

'Perhaps' she agreed, 'Anyway the beautiful swans spied the Ugly Duckling first, and began to swim towards him'

'What did he do?' asked Ryan.

'The Ugly Duckling felt so bad that he just bowed his head in shame'

At that point the Cantadora started to gather up her belongings as if to leave.

'As usual!' thought Ryan ruefully 'Stopping just at the interesting bit!'

'We'll talk some more next time' she began.

'No, wait!' interrupted Ryan suddenly. 'I remember

this bit!.... When he bowed his head towards the water, he saw his reflection'

'Aha! You've remembered! And what did he see there?'

'He saw that he wasn't really an Ugly Duckling after all'

'Well done, Ryan!' she clapped. 'You've remembered'

'Yes, I do remember. The Ugly Duckling had grown into a beautiful swan'

'Indeed he had!' agreed the Cantadora. 'So beautiful that people admired him everywhere he went'

The Cantadora looked closely at Ryan. For the second time that day, there were tears in his eyes.

'That's the end of the story, isn't it?' he said.

'Why are you sad, Ryan?' she asked gently. 'It's a happy ending, isn't it?'

'Yes, but now you'll never come back to see me'

'Why would I do that?'

'Because story is finished'

'Of course I'll come back! We still have to find the story's treasure, don't forget!'

'Its treasure? Oh, yeah, you mean the hidden message' said Ryan, remembering. 'But how will we do that?'

The Cantadora laughed.

'Have patience, Ryan!' she said. 'You know what I always say'

'Yeah' he said, smiling in spite of himself. 'Treasure seeking is not to be rushed!'

The following day, Kev was back in school. With Kev beside him things improved in class for Ryan. He even managed to keep out of trouble with Miss Neill. So even though he had still heard nothing from Nick, life seemed better. Ryan began to think that maybe things weren't so bad after all.

Unfortunately he couldn't have been more wrong.

That weekend some serious news broke - news that was to upset not only Ryan, but the entire school as well.

Mum and Dad called the boys together when they heard.

'Do you know a boy from your school called Kev Shepherd?' asked Mum solemnly.

'Yeah' answered Danny. 'That's the boy who sits beside Ryan'

'Well, I'm afraid he's been attacked' she said.

'What happened?' asked Danny, shocked.

'The Police aren't sure. He was found unconscious in a house in Belmont Road'

'Is he dead?' asked Ryan.

'No. But apparently he's seriously injured. He's in a coma in Belmont hospital'

Mum didn't know much more than that, so she couldn't give the boys any other information. But she did give them all sorts of warnings about being careful.

'I thought this was a safe neighbourhood' she said in disbelief.

Dad was in a state of shock.

'I can't believe anyone would attack a youngster like that. It's disgusting!'

'There's going to be no more walking home from school for you two boys' said Mum. 'And no more wandering off on your own, Ryan. Do you hear me?'

'OK, Mum' they both promised.

On Monday the whole school was buzzing with the news. All sorts of rumours were flying around:

'Did you hear about Kevin Shepherd?'
'They say he may not survive'
'I heard he's got serious brain injuries'
'They say the Belmont Burglar did it!'

Ryan was very shaken by all he heard, and took to his room where he stayed for hours without speaking to a soul. Mum was getting more worried about him by the day - He didn't seem to even want to talk about Kev.

She decided to ring the Cantadora for advice.

'Apperently Kev Shepherd has befriended him at school recently' Mum said. 'He must be so upset about what has happened, but he refuses to speak'

'He's probably heard all sorts of rumours' the Cantadora guessed accurately. 'Talk to him. He needs facts at the moment, not rumours and exaggerations'

So that evening Mum took Ryan aside and told him truthfully what she had been able to find out.

'Apparently Kev lives alone with his grandfather. While his grandfather was out someone came into the house and attacked Kev'

'But why would someone attack Kevin?' asked Ryan, puzzled.

'You need to know this, Ryan - There is someone prowling around our neighbourhood at the moment – someone who's up to no good'

'You mean the Belmont Burglar?'

Even Ryan had heard about the Belmont Burglar by that time.

'Yes, the Belmont Burglar, as they call him. It looks very much like he's the one who attacked Kev. The Police think Kev disturbed him while he was stealing from his grandfather's house'

Ryan, as you know was a boy with very firm views on things like right and wrong and good and bad. Burglars were bad in anybody's book. But anyone who would attack Kevin was even worse.

He lay awake that night, thinking about the person who had attacked his friend, his heart brimming with hatred.

'I'll get even with the Belmont Burglar' he swore to himself.

He wasn't sure how yet. He just knew he'd find a way.

Little did Ryan know that the person he was swearing to get even with was none other than Nick Kelly - the 'friend' he had been so longing to hear from.

Chapter 10

POLICE INVESTIGATION

That night while the rest of the family were sound asleep, Ryan lay in bed awake, his mind racing as usual. Eventually he sneaked out of bed and turned on the light. And even though he still hadn't found his 'Cantadora Pen', he began a new List in his Secret Journal:

Getting even with the Belmont Burglar, who attacked Kevin Shepherd
List of Ideas
   1) *First track him down (problem - how?)*
   2) *Assist the Police Investigation (problem – am I too young?)*

He was a bit stuck after that, but the next morning another idea came to him.

'Nick would know what to do' he thought. 'Gangsters must have ways of tracking down burglars - If only I could find Nick!'

So he added a third idea to his list:

---

   3) *Find Nick and get his help to track down the Belmont Burglar*
       (problem – where is Nick?)

But finding Nick seemed impossible at the moment. For one thing, Mum would hardly allow Danny or him out of the house, while the Belmont Burglar was on the loose. And for another, Nick Kelly was in hiding, and he had had no intention of contacting Ryan of all people.

Mum was no help when he tried to talk to her the following day.

'There's nothing a kid like you can do' she said dismissively.

'I'm sure I could look for clues or something'

'Don't be silly, Ryan' she said. 'This is a matter for the Police'

'Maybe I could be their Secret Agent or something'

'Oh, for heaven's sake, Ryan!'

'I could. I know a lot about being a Secret Agent. Honest!'

'Look, Ryan, this is not a game. You are to stay in the house and put these silly ideas out of your head'

'But Mum…'

'That's enough, Ryan! I realise you're upset about Kevin, but this is no matter for a kid to get involved in'

'My main problem', he decided later with a sigh, 'is that adults don't take me seriously enough'

Little did he know, but he was soon to be taken very seriously indeed - As soon as the following day, in fact.

Ryan was watching TV with Mum, Dad and Maria when all of a sudden Danny came bursting into the room.

'A Police Car has pulled up outside our house' he yelled.

'No way, Danny!' said Maria, as she and Ryan jumped up to look out the window.

'I bet it's something to do with Kev Shepherd' she said.

Mum made her way to the front door, which she

opened to reveal the towering figures of two burly policemen.

'Is this the home of a Ryan Jeremy Gillespie' asked the taller of the two.

'Oh, my goodness!' said Maria, sounding impressed. 'They're looking for you, Ryan. I wonder what they want'

As Mum and Dad showed them in, the taller policeman introduced himself as Detective Bennett and his colleague as Detective Fox. Then, for what seemed like ages, Ryan and Danny pressed their ears to the kitchen door while Mum and Dad talked to the Policemen. Unfortunately they couldn't make out what was being said.

Eventually the door opened and Dad came into the hallway with Detective Bennett, looking very serious.

'Ryan, the Police Officers would like to have a word with you'

Ryan's heart missed a beat.

'It's Kevin. He's dead, isn't he?' he said.

'No, son. He's not dead'

'Then why do they want to talk to me?' Ryan asked

Detective Bennett eyed Ryan curiously before speaking.

'We've found something belonging to you, Ryan' he said.

'To me?' he repeated. 'What is it?'

The Detective reached into his pocket and withdrew a gold parker pen. Holding it aloft, he read from the barrel:

'*Ryan Jeremy Gillespie*'

'It's my Cantadora Pen!' exclaimed Ryan, delighted.

'Do you know where we found it?'

'No, where?'

'It was lying in the back porch of a house'

'Oh?' said Ryan.

'Don't you want to know where the house was?'

'Where?'

'Belmont Park Avenue. Do you know it?'

'Yeah' said Ryan.

'Of course I do', he thought proudly. 'I know practically every street in the neighbourhood!'

'Have you any idea how it got there?' asked the Detective.

Ryan paused for a moment before he answered. He was puzzled. Why were the Police making all this fuss over a pen, he wondered. Surely they had more important things to do. Like hunting down the Belmont Burglar!

He considered whether he should say this, but decided not to. It might sound rude, he figured, especially when they had been kind enough to return his pen to him.

'Ryan' repeated the Detective, 'have you any idea how it got there?'

Ryan shrugged.

'I suppose I must have dropped it' he said eventually.

As you know, Ryan had been unable to hear the conversation that had just taken place between his parents and the Police. If he had heard it, he would have been very worried indeed.

As soon as Mum and Dad showed them in, Detective

Bennett asked them to identify Ryan's pen. Then he told them it had been found lying at the scene of one of the recent robberies.

'My goodness!' said Mum. 'How on earth did Ryan's pen get there?'

'That's what we're trying to establish. It looks like it was dropped and rolled behind a table'

'Dropped? Who would have dropped it'

'Probably Ryan himself'

Mum and Dad were completely at a loss.

'Why on earth would Ryan be in a house on Belmont Park Avenue?'

Detective Bennett heaved a sigh before he continued.

'We're still completing our investigations, Mrs Gillespie, but I have to be honest with you, things don't look good'

'What do you mean?'

'Well, we have been investigating the recent spate of robberies in the area'

'You mean the Belmont Burglar'

'Exactly. In the course of our enquiries, several residents have reported unusual activities on their property'

'Unusual activities?' Mum repeated.

'Yes, Reports of an intruder - a certain youth who has been climbing over garden walls and in and out of houses'

'A certain youth?'

Detective Bennett sighed. He had been dreading this bit.

'Mr and Mrs Gillespie' he said heavily, 'I'm afraid the

descriptions we've received of the intruder match your son Ryan exactly'

But since Ryan had heard none of this conversation, he had no idea he was under any suspicion.

'Ryan' Dad asked in a very solemn tone, 'is there anything you'd like to say to the Policeman?'

'Oh, sorry' said Ryan. He thought Dad meant he had forgotten his manners. 'Thanks for returning my pen'

'Things aren't so bad after all', Ryan thought. 'Kevin is still alive. And I have my found my Cantadora Pen!'

Not for a moment did he suspect what serious trouble he was in.

Chapter 11

THE BELMONT
BURGLAR

It wasn't till Mum started to cry that Ryan realised that something was badly wrong.

'Mr & Mrs Gillespie' said Detective Bennett, 'I know we don't have a search warrant, but if we have your permission, we'd like to take a look round your son's room'

'Absolutely!' said Dad. 'We're as keen as you are to get to the bottom of all this'

'Look round my room?' repeated Ryan, outraged. 'What for? They don't have MY permission'

But Detectives Bennett and Fox ignored him, and made their way to his bedroom.

As they were carrying out their search, Mum and Dad took Ryan to one side and explained to him exactly what was going on. Slowly, the awful truth began to sink in.

'I'm in *big* trouble this time' he realised with a shock. 'They think *I* am the Belmont Burglar!'

But instead of opening up and telling them the truth, Ryan went completely silent, and refused to answer any of the questions that were put to him. No one could get a word out of him for the rest of the evening.

The stolen goods that the Detectives were hoping to find for were of course nowhere to be found. But just as they were finishing their search, Detective Fox found something else under Ryan's bed. It was his Address List.

'Take a look at this!' he said, handing it over to his colleague. 'It's a list of just about every street in the Belmont area'

Bennett let out a low whistle.

'Unbelievable!' he replied. 'The kid looks like butter wouldn't melt in his mouth. But from this it looks like he planned the whole thing from his bedroom'

And he carefully folded Ryan's Address List and removed it as evidence.

'Looks like we've found our Belmont Burglar' said Fox. 'A kid! Who would have believed it?'

From that moment on, Mum seemed to do nothing but cry and talk to Dad for hours about what had gone wrong.

'It's all my fault' she wailed. 'I should have kept a closer eye on him. I should never have let him go out on his own like that'

'It's my fault too' said Dad. 'I just assumed he was going for walks. It never crossed my mind that he up to anything'

'Where on earth will he end up' she cried, 'if he's in trouble with the Police at his age?'

'I can hardly believe it' Dad said sadly. 'I know he's been in trouble in school a lot. But I never thought anything like this would happen'

'Where did we go wrong?' they asked each other.

Unfortunately just about everything pointed to Ryan's guilt - especially the discovery of the Cantadora Pen. One lady had even managed to get a photo of Ryan using her mobile phone. It was the lady who had turned the water hose on him one evening. Detective Bennett asked Mum and Dad to have a look at the photo; and even though it was of poor quality and taken from behind, they had no doubt whatsoever that the figure flying across her lawn that evening was none other than their son.

Mum remembered being puzzled the evening Ryan had come home soaked through.

'I didn't know it was raining, son' she had commented, before putting the matter out of her head. But now, when she remembered the incident, she bowed her head and began to sob.

There was no point in looking to Ryan for explanations at the moment, because he barely came out of his room and was still refusing to speak. Somehow it didn't occur to him to utter the words 'It wasn't me'. Who knows why? – Partly because he was had spent a lifetime getting into trouble perhaps - often without quite understanding the reason. This kind of thing was nothing new to him, though the trouble had never been as serious before. And as usual no one seemed to doubt his guilt.

You see, when Ryan was going through one of his quiet spells, no one had much idea what he was thinking. At the moment he hardly knew himself, but he had never in his life before felt more scared and confused.

The Police had refused to give him back his Cantadora Pen, much to his disappointment, but he took his Secret Journal out of the jacket pocket and read it all over many times. It was about the only thing that seemed to make sense at the moment.

At last, slowly he began to write:

<u>*Facing Facts*</u>
>   *I, Ryan Gillespie am being falsely accused of being*
>   *the Belmont Burglar.*

Then, with a heavy sigh, he began writing a new list. Here's what he wrote:

<u>*List of Evidence Against Myself, Ryan Gillespie*</u>
1)   *My Cantadora Pen was found at the scene of crime.*
2)   *Witnesses saw me behaving suspiciously.*
3)   *My Address List was found in my room.*
4)   *I often went for walks on my own*
5)   *I have no alibi*

The more often Ryan read this over, the more damning it looked. Then below his 'List of Evidence, he wrote:

<u>*Sequence of Events which have led up to this*</u>
1)   *My twin brother, Danny Gillespie threatened my life*
2)   *No one offered me ANY protection. Not even my own parents!*
3)   *My friend, Nick Kelly (2nd best) was the only person who listened to me and agreed to protect my life. He is the only person who knows I am innocent - but he is nowhere to be found.*
4)   *Although I did sneak in to houses and gardens I did not do anything bad. It was only for the games I played with Nick, ie*
     A.   the Secret Agent Game, or
     B.   the Key Game

By the way, on the subject of sneaking in to people's houses, I should explain that Ryan had come to realise - only now, when it was too late - how that was a very wrong thing to do. You might find yourself wondering how on earth he could have been so stupid as to not realise before. But, as we know, Ryan found some things hard to figure out. Yes, of course he knew it was against the law. But when Nick told him it was just a game, Ryan believed him.

You see, in Ryan's mind there were some laws that had to be obeyed and other laws that could be ignored. He had figured this out years ago, once when he was a very small boy. It was one day while he was out with Dad. A group of teenagers were playing football outside the corner shop, even though Ryan could read a big sign in full view:

'NO BALL GAMES' it said. *'BY ORDER OF THE COUNCIL'*

Ryan had run straight over.

'Can you not read the sign?' he yelled angrily.

As usual Ryan had only got laughed at for his efforts, so Dad took him to the side and talked patiently to him.

'They are only having a bit of fun, Ryan'

'But, Dad, it's against the law. Did you not see the sign?'

'Lighten up, son' he said. 'Sometimes it's OK to break the law a bit'

'Is it?' asked Ryan, surprised.

'Yes. Just as long as no one's getting hurt and people are having fun'

Years later, when Nick was asking him to play their 'games', Ryan had remembered what Dad had told him, word for word.

'It's OK' he told himself. 'Just as long as no one's getting hurt and people are having fun'

Some part of Ryan longed to tell the whole story, from his point of view, but he remained silent. He was very used to keeping his private thoughts to himself.

'So the Police think I'm the Belmont Burglar?' he thought bitterly. 'Well, let them think whatever they want. I don't care'

Chapter 12 _____

Family In Shock

Of course the truth is that Ryan *did* care. He cared very much indeed. No one likes to be falsely accused. And he had no idea what the future held for him now that he was branded a thief. He did realise that he could end up going to jail though….and he had thought Freak School sounded bad!

Even though Ryan realised there was a lot of evidence against him, it was still horrible to feel that no one in the world believed he was innocent. Nick was the only person who could have helped clear his name, but Nick had gone away. And anyway he had promised Nick never to give away their secrets, and Ryan liked to keep his promises.

By this stage, he had no doubt that Nick must still be Pakistan, no matter what Ivan had said. In Ryan's mind, if Nick had been in town he would have been in touch by now. So unless Nick happened to come home, the situation was hopeless. As the days went by, Ryan became more and more unhappy.

And he was not the only one. The whole Gillespie family were in a state of shock about what had happened. Nobody seemed even to be having proper conversations any more - although Mum and Dad did a lot of talking in hushed tones, behind closed doors.

Meal times were the worst. Every time a meal was ready, Ryan said he was not hungry. Mum insisted that he at least come to the table and try to eat something, but usually he took no more than a couple of forkfuls before disappearing off to his room again and closing the door.

Sometimes Dad tried to break the awkward silence and strike up a conversation. But even an innocent remark could lead to a row, as he was soon to find out.

'Did anyone see the newspaper I was reading earlier?' he asked.

No one answered. Mum was just staring into space.

'I'm sure I left it on the coffee table' he went on. 'Did anyone see it?'

In the end it was Danny who broke the silence.

'Have you searched the thief's room? Your paper's probably there'

'DANNY!' said Dad crossly. 'There's no need for that kind of talk'

'It's true! He is a thief. You and Mum won't talk about it, but you know it's true as well'

By this time, Ryan had rushed from the table.

'Ryan!' Mum called after him. 'Come back here and finish your meal'

But it was no use. Ryan was already in his room with the door slammed behind him and there was no way he was coming out. He had heard enough to confirm what he already knew. No one in his family trusted him. They believed he was just a common thief.

But the worst thing of all for Ryan was this - he was sure his own parents thought he was guilty - and that they hated him for it.

And in one way he was right. How could his parents come to any conclusion other than that their son was guilty? The evidence was impossible to ignore. And Ryan was doing nothing to protest his innocence.

Yet in another way he was wrong. His parents didn't hate him. They were just very shocked and confused. But he was still their son, no matter what he had done. There was no use lecturing him or punishing him. Things had got beyond that stage.

If Ryan had been able to hear some of their private conversations during those long days after the Police visit, he would have heard sadness and concern in their voices, but not hatred.

'I still can't believe it' Mum kept saying.

'I know, love. It's a dreadful shock'

'I feel like my own son's a stranger these days' she said, with tears in her eyes. 'I don't even know what to say to him'

'He's not a bad boy' Dad reassured her. 'He just needs professional help'

'Professional help?' repeated Mum. 'Look how many people have tried over the years. Nobody has been much help so far'

'I know, but this is different. They'll have to take us seriously now'

'Yeah' said Mum bitterly. 'I'm sure he'll get the best professional help available when he's in juvenile prison'

Dad was startled at the harshness in her voice, but when he looked into her eyes he could see the pain it was masking.

'Try not to worry, Nancy. It will be OK in the end' he said gently.

'I don't see how' she replied. And for the umpteenth time recently she burst into tears.

Ryan didn't know it yet, but there was one person in the family who refused to believe he was guilty. And that was his sister, Maria. She had tried to discuss the matter with Mum a few times and ended up getting nowhere.

'I don't care what everyone says, Mum' Maria told her. 'Ryan's not a thief'

'I know how you feel, Maria. He's your brother. You want to believe he's innocent. We all do. But it's an open and shut case. The Police have even got photographs'

'And what about Kev Shepherd? Do the Police think Ryan attacked him too?'

'I don't know'

'Oh, come on, Mum. There's no way Ryan would do something like that. There has to be some other explanation'

'Like what?'

'What if he was set up or something?'

'Who by?'

'I don't know. One of his friends maybe?'

Mum sighed.

'What friends, Maria? You know he hardly bothers with anyone'

'Did he not mention some friend recently? Remember once he said he'd lost a friend's phone number?'

Unfortunately the conversation didn't go any further, because Mum said she had enough to cope with at the moment without arguing with Maria.

But Maria wouldn't let it go. And even though Ryan would hardly utter a word these days (and no one was talking to him much either) she took it on herself to try and get him to open up to her.

She went to his bedroom door and gave a knock. There was no reply.

'Ryan!' she called. 'Ryan!'

Still no answer.

'Ryan, can I come in?'

Again she was met with silence.

And when she tried to open the door Ryan held it closed from the other side.

'Ryan I'm going to keep knocking your door till you let me in. I don't care how long it takes'

It took nearly half an hour of patient knocking and calling before Ryan finally opened the door. But he wedged his foot against it, so Maria couldn't get in.

'What do you want?' he asked grumpily.

Maria wasn't sure what to reply.

'Ryan, I know you really want to be left on your own at the moment' she said. 'But I'm your sister and I love you. I hate to see you unhappy like this'

Ryan just stared at the floor.

'I just wish you would open up with me' she said with a heavy sigh.

For a few moments neither of them spoke.

'Look, Ryan, I know you would never do something bad. I know you are innocent'

At last Ryan looked her in the eye. Those were the very words he needed to hear. At last he opened the door and let her in.

Funny enough, once Maria was in Ryan's room, she'd no idea what to say next. In her mind, Ryan was innocent, and there had to be an explanation for everything. She was also convinced that Ryan would tell it to her, if only she could get him to open up. But she'd no idea how to get through to him.

For a while she did all the talking.

'Ryan, things look bad against you. I really want to help you prove your innocence. But I can't unless you tell me things from your point of view'

She was getting fed up being met with silence.

'Ryan, please. Just tell me what's going on'

More silence.

'RYAN!' she yelled in exasperation. 'I'm trying to HELP you and I don't think you're even listening to me'

Maria was right actually. He wasn't really listening. But what Maria didn't realise was that although Ryan wanted to listen, he was finding it very hard. Ever since the Police visit he had been doing his Tooth Tapping constantly - and somehow now he could barely stop long enough to pay attention to something else.

Suddenly she had a brainwave.

'Ryan, would you like to go and visit Kev in hospital?'

It was the breakthrough she needed. Ryan stopped his Tooth Tapping for a moment.

'Yes, please, Maria. I'd love to'

Chapter 13

VISITING WARD 15

The idea of bringing Ryan to visit Kev had come to Maria out of the blue. But she could see at once that it would mean a lot to Ryan, so she promised to take him up to Belmont hospital the next day. What she hadn't counted on, however was that Mum and Dad would not be so keen on the idea.

'You've decided to do *what*?' yelled Mum, when Maria mentioned it later.

'Mum, I'm sure it would cheer him up. You should have seen his face when I mentioned it'

'It's out of the question' said Mum, with a note of finality in her voice.

'But Mum, I promised Ryan…'

'Maria' said Dad more gently. 'You must understand. Ryan is the last person that the Shepherd family want to see at the moment'

'How do you know that? Have you ever spoken to them?'

'No, we don't know the family at all. I only know that Ryan's parents died when he was small and that he's been raised by his grandfather. The old man must have enough on his plate at the moment worrying about Kevin being in a coma. It would only upset him to come face to face with….'

'Face to face with what?' Maria butted in angrily. 'With a criminal? Or with his friend who obviously cares about him?'

The argument continued in the same vein for another while until all of a sudden Mum broke down and began to sob.

'Look, Maria' explained her Dad. 'Your Mum is under a lot of pressure at the moment. You must understand that. Let it go now. We can talk about it some other time'

Feeling very frustrated, Maria went on to bed - but not before she had looked in on Ryan again.

'Ryan' she whispered as he opened the door. 'I'm going to knock your door tomorrow morning at half past nine. I know you hate getting up early on Saturday mornings, but you have to get ready without a fuss so we can sneak out quietly'

'Why have we to sneak out?' he asked.

'Mum and Dad mustn't know we're going'

'Why not?'

'I'll explain in the morning. Now goodnight!' she said.

The next morning Maria and Ryan slipped quietly out of the house as planned, before anyone else was up, and made their way to the local café for breakfast. And even though Ryan was very quiet, Maria thought he seemed to be quite enjoying the adventure!

'You seem to be in good form' she remarked.

He didn't answer. But at least he's looking happier, thought Maria, as she watched him chomp his way through his bacon and egg.

'Ryan' she asked later, after they'd taken their seats on the bus, 'do you remember I said last night I'd love to help you?'

Ryan nodded.

'Well, I can't unless you talk to me'

Ryan just blinked and looked out of the window. He longed for help of course. But he knew he couldn't break his promise and tell her about Nick, so there was no point in saying anything at all.

'Ryan' persisted Maria later. 'Please.... just say *something*'

Ryan thought for a moment before replying.

'Why do Mum and Dad not know we're going to the hospital?' he asked.

'They think Kev's family might prefer him only to have visitors who are family'

'I suppose the Police told them I'm the Belmont Burglar and they hate me. It's not fair'

'So talk to me and let me help you clear your name!'

But again he refused to reply, leaving her completely exasperated.

Now at Maria's age, one thing she really hated was being lectured at. Nevertheless right now she found herself thinking that a good lecture might be just what Ryan needed. So she decided to give it a try.

'Look, Ryan, there's no point in saying people hate you and feeling sorry for yourself' she barked. 'What are people expected to think? You sneaked off round people's houses and now you're refusing to say a word to explain yourself. Maybe you'd have an easier time if you weren't always so rude and unfriendly'

'I'm not always rude and unfriendly' protested Ryan.

'You are actually' she muttered.

Ryan looked really upset.

'How am I?' he asked.

'Is that supposed to be a serious question, Ryan?'

'Yes, it is' he replied in a small voice. 'I'm fed up with people saying things like that about me'

Sighing heavily, Maria decided that maybe the time was right for a few home truths.

'Look, I'm going to be honest with you here, Ryan. You really *do* come across as rude and unfriendly'

'But how? What is it I'm doing wrong?'

'Just about everything really. It's like you go around in a world of your own. I mean you don't even speak to people unless you feel like it. Half the time you don't even bother looking at them! You only take an interest in what *you* want to. Sometimes the way you say things can be really blunt and offputting....'

Ryan didn't want to hear any more.

'You must hate me too if you think I do all that!' he interrupted.

'I *don't* hate you, Ryan' said Maria. 'I just wish you'd wise up sometimes'

'What do you mean?'

'Use your head a bit. Like now for example. We'll probably meet some of Kev's family. Why don't you try being friendly? You know. Smile. Ask how Kevin is. All that kind of thing'

Ryan thought it over.

'Will you make an effort at least?' she persisted.

'OK, I'll try' he said.

'Promise?'

'OK'

'You mean it, Ryan?'

'Yes'

And at that precise moment Ryan really did mean it! He was determined to show Maria that he was not 'rude and unfriendly'. He also wanted to make a good impression on Kevin's family. In fact it was so important to him that he reached into his pocket to get out his Secret Journal. He knew he had a better chance of remembering it if he wrote it down.

'Have you got a pen?' he asked Maria.

'No, sorry. I haven't…. What on earth are you writing anyway, Ryan?'

'Important lists and things!' he replied indignantly.

Maria laughed.

'Well, we've no time anyway. We need to get off the bus now. Here's the hospital'

Sure enough, they had arrived. After finding their way to reception, Maria managed to find out from the lady at Reception that Kevin Shepherd was in Ward 15.

'It's along that direction' she said pointing. 'You'll have to speak to the nurse'

'Thanks for your help' Ryan said to her.

Maria was impressed at his manners. At least he's making an effort, she thought smiling.

At the entrance to Ward 15, Maria spoke politely to the nurse, explaining who they were and why they had come.

'Just wait here' she said. 'Kevin's grandfather is with him at the moment. I'll have a word'

During the five minutes or so that they had to wait, Ryan's heart began to race. He was trying hard to think of ways to be polite and friendly, but there was something about the tiny flicker of the fluorescent lighting above their heads that was getting to him. His mind started to wander off.

No one can help me except Nick, he thought for the umpteenth time. If only Nick would come home from Pakistan and hear about my troubles. In Ryan's mind, Nick was still his only hope.

He noticed himself Tooth Tapping again.

'I must stop that' he told himself. 'What was it the Cantadora suggested for when I can't stop myself from Tooth Tapping?'

Then he remembered.

'Concentrate on something else when that happens' she had said. 'Listen to music maybe. Or look out the window'

Ryan took a few steps over to the window and forced himself to look out. The courtyard was empty except for one man who was leaning against the railings near the entranceway, smoking. From the back, there was something a bit familiar about him.

Just at that a slim, neatly dressed, white haired man approached them.

'Hello' he said reaching out his hand towards Maria. 'I'm Jim. Kevin's grandfather'

'Pleased to meet you' said Maria. He seems a nice old man, she thought. There was something about the twinkle in his eye that made her take to him right away.

'Thank-you so much for coming. It's very kind of you' he said.

So Mum and Dad were wrong, Maria thought triumphantly. Kev's grandfather isn't upset to see us at all. He couldn't be more warm and friendly.

'How's Kev?' she asked.

'Just the same really' replied Jim. 'Still in a coma. We won't really know how he is until he comes out of it'

'Oh, I hope he'll be OK' said Maria.

Jim looked over at Ryan who was still staring out of the window.

'So this is young Ryan?' asked Jim.

'Ryan!' called Maria. 'This is Jim, Kevin's grandfather'

But Ryan didn't respond. Maria stepped over and gave him a nudge.

'Ryan!' she hissed. 'Will you come and say hello to Kev's grandfather'

What happened next took both Maria and Jim completely by surprise. With no warning whatsoever, Ryan suddenly took off! Without a word he took to his heels and ran towards the hospital entrance as fast as his legs would carry him. Maria was to say later that she'd never felt more embarrassed in her life.

'I'm sorry, Jim' she said. 'I'm afraid I'll have to go after him'

She had no idea what on earth was going on. But one thing was for sure. She was going to find out!

Chapter 14

MISPLACED TRUST

Ever since Maria had mentioned the idea of going to visit Kev, Ryan had been able to think of little else. Then during the bus journey, when Maria told him bluntly how 'rude and unfriendly' he was, he didn't like it. He hoped Kev's family wouldn't think that way about him. So he resolved to make a big effort to be friendly while they were at the hospital.

So what had happened to put all that right out of his head, and cause him to go flying off without a word, leaving Maria and Jim standing bewildered in the corridor?

It was the man he had been watching through the window. Each time he took a drag from his cigarette, somehow it reminded Ryan of Nick. It seemed like Ryan couldn't get Nick out of his head these days.

'Nick was the only person who cared when Danny threatened to kill me' he thought fondly.

Then just at the moment when the man flicked his butt into the gutter and turned to walk off towards the hospital gates that Ryan realised. It *was* Nick!... Or was it? .... Ryan couldn't be certain, but it certainly looked like him. And in that moment everything else left his mind. He simply had to dash out and see Nick, before he disappeared out of sight again.

By the time Ryan made it to the hospital gates, Nick was nowhere to be seen. Ryan looked up and down the street frantically, unsure which direction to turn. Then he caught a glimpse of him on the far side of the road. At the far side of the pedestrian crossing, he began to run again. As he ran, he was happily picturing himself catching up and tugging Nick's sleeve. Wouldn't Nick get a surprise when he turned round? Ryan could hardly wait.

Just at that, Nick headed off down a side street, and Ryan was afraid he might lose sight of him again.

'NICK!' he yelled at the top of his voice. 'NICK!'

For a split second 'Nick' stopped and glanced over his shoulder. The two of them barely made eye contact. Then just as quickly, he turned away and started walking, this time more smartly.

'NICK!' Ryan yelled again. 'It's me! I need to talk to you!'

Ryan kept running. But when he got to the corner of the street that Nick had turned down, there was no sign of him. Ryan raced up and down several times, checking at every turn off and yelling Nick's name.

In the end he had to give up. He could hear Maria calling him, but he couldn't bring himself to answer her. When she eventually found him, he was sitting on the kerb, his head buried in his hands.

'Ryan!' she yelled. 'What on earth are you up to?'

He didn't even raise his head.

'Why did you go and do a runner? We came all that way to visit Kev and now you've gone and messed it all up'

Ryan still didn't move. She poked him in the side with her foot.

'Come on' she said crossly. 'We're going home now'

It was only when he pulled himself heavily to his feet and she saw his face that she realised he had been crying. But he would not speak during the entire journey home, so she had no way of knowing what was wrong.

For the rest of the day Ryan refused to come out of his room, but that evening when the doorbell rang, he came down the stairs. He was expecting the Cantadora, so a look of shock came over his face when he opened the door to reveal an old man with white hair.

'Hello, Ryan. Do you remember me? I'm Jim, Kevin's grandfather. I've come for a word with your Mum and Dad'

Ryan wished the earth would open up and swallow him. If Mum and Dad hadn't heard how he behaved at the hospital earlier, they were sure going to now. It served him right, he supposed, but he wished the old man hadn't come round to complain. As Ryan took to his heels and ran to his room again, he overheard Jim introducing himself to Mum, and Mum asking him would he like to come in.

Ten minutes later, Maria knocked on his door.

'Did you not hear the doorbell, Ryan? The Cantadora is here'

Ryan poked his head out.

'What's Kevin's grandfather doing here?'

'I honestly don't know, Ryan. He's talking to Mum and Dad in the back room…. But look, forget him for now. The Cantadora is waiting for you'

The Cantadora was well aware of the problems Ryan was facing at the moment. The two of them played cards as usual that evening, but she could tell that Ryan's heart wasn't in it.

'You know what, Ryan?' she said eventually. 'I think you're ready to find the Treasure tonight'

'You mean the hidden message in the Ugly Duckling story?'

'Exactly'

'How do we do that?'

'It's very simple. All you need to do is search your heart'

Ryan looked puzzled.

'Well, your heart is hurting a lot at the moment. Am I right?'

He just shrugged.

'And do you remember how the Ugly Duckling felt?'

When Ryan answered, the Cantadora was surprised at how passionately he spoke.

'Yes, I remember' he said 'He felt ugly - and sad - and horrible - and stupid - and lonely - and ashamed!'

'That's right. And the reason you can understand how he felt so well is because *you* feel all those things right now, don't you?'

'So what if I do?' said Ryan bitterly. 'How does that help us find the hidden message?'

'Think what happened next, Ryan….. What happened when the Ugly Duckling got to his lowest point?'

'He looked down and saw his reflection in the water'

'Yes, and he had turned into a beautiful swan!'

'So what's the hidden message then?'

'This is the message - *You* are the beautiful swan, Ryan. At the moment you still think you're like an Ugly Duckling. You feel like you are different, people don't like you, and you don't fit in anywhere. But soon things will change. Soon you will see your true reflection. You will find other swans. And when you do, you will feel much happier'

'Is that it?' said Ryan, unimpressed.

'That's it'

'It's not much of a message'

'Why's that?'

'OK, maybe I do feel like an Ugly Duckling. But it's just a stupid story, and I'm not going to turn into a swan some day!'

That night after the rest of the family had gone to bed, Ryan was lying awake as usual. He couldn't understand why the Cantadora had let him down like that, with her stupid 'hidden message' - treating him like some dopey kid! As if he was going to waken up in the morning and discover he had grown wings or something.

He was really disappointed. He had really been looking forward to finding the hidden message. And it just turned out to be babyish nonsense. What a let down! …And he couldn't understand why Nick had ignored him today either. Was there *anyone* he could trust not to let him down, he wondered.

He took his Secret Journal out of his jacket pocket, turned to a fresh page, and began to write. Here's what he wrote:

<u>Problem – Deciding who I can really trust</u>
List of Possibilities

<u>Possibility 1- Mum and Dad?</u>
Reasons to trust Mum and Dad -
1. They are my parents
2. They are kind to me

Reasons not to trust Mum and Dad -
1. Not all parents can be trusted.
2. They did not care when Danny threatened to kill me
3. They are planning to send me away to Freak School.

<u>Possibility 2- Danny?</u>
Reasons to trust Danny -
1. He's my brother

Reasons not to trust Danny
1. Not all siblings can be trusted.
2. He's always mean to me
3. He threatened to kill me (main reason)

<u>Possibility 3- Maria?</u>
Reasons to trust Maria -
1. She's my sister
2. She's usually very kind to me

Reasons not to trust Maria -
1. Not all siblings can be trusted.
2. She did not protect me when Danny threatened to kill me

Possibility 4- The Cantadora?
Reasons to trust the Cantadora -
1. She is very kind

Reasons not to trust the Cantadora -
1. Sometimes she expects me to believe babyish stuff
   – like that I will turn into a swan!
2. Sometimes she tells me stupid stuff like that people
   can be very powerful, like the sun, without being
   forceful and mean

Possibility 5- Nick Kelly?
Reasons to trust Nick-
1. He has been very kind to me.
2. He protected me when Danny threatened my life.

Reasons not to trust Nick-

He was about to write down his reason not to trust Nick
– that he had ignored him that day.

Then, just before he did so, he changed his mind. For
one thing he wasn't 100% certain it was Nick. But even
if it was, Ryan suddenly remembered what Nick had told
him about undercover agents.

'If they meet by accident, they might have to pretend
they don't know each other' Nick had said.

'That's IT!' Ryan decided. 'I knew there had to be a
good reason why Nick ignored me!'

So in Ryan's mind now there was no longer any reason
not to trust Nick.

'Nick will help me clear my name. All I need to is

find him!'

And so, at the end of his 'List of Possibilities' he added the following:

Decision – The only person I can trust is Nick Kelly!

After that he lay tossing and turning for another five minutes. Then very quickly and quietly he pulled on some clothes, opened his bedroom window and climbed out into the darkness.

Chapter 15

SHOCK DISCOVERIES

Normally Maria slept like a log. But that night she was having problems getting to sleep too. She hadn't told Mum and Dad about their trip to the hospital earlier, because she knew they would only give off - and they didn't ask about it anyway. Kev's grandfather had stayed for quite a while talking to them. But even after he left, Mum and Dad still didn't mention it. Maria almost wished they would hurry up and tell her off - at least that would get it over with!

She was finally dropping off to sleep when she heard a sound. Listening carefully, she recognised the click of a window catch. Then she heard someone jump down onto the patio.

It's Ryan!' she realised, sitting bolt upright. 'He must be running away'

For a moment she wondered if she should waken Mum and Dad, but then she thought better of it. Climbing out of bed as quietly as she could, she made her way to Ryan's room.

As she suspected, his bed was empty and the window open. Maria rushed back to her own room, pulled on her slippers and threw a jacket over her clothes. Then, rather than risk wakening anyone else by going downstairs, she decided to climb out of Ryan's window after him.

It was just as she was doing so that she noticed his red notebook lying at the edge of his bed. Without quite knowing why, she picked it up and stuffed it into the inside pocket of her jacket.

It wasn't hard to find him at that time of night, for there was nobody else about, and she could see him walking briskly along the street. At first she followed at a distance, curious about where he might go. Before long she realised he was following the bus route that they'd taken earlier that day. Perhaps he's decided to go to the hospital again, she thought. How weird!

Eventually she decided to catch up with him.

'Ryan!' she called, quickening her pace.

He looked back in surprise, and immediately began to run from her.

'Ryan, stop! Where are you going?' she called.

But Ryan just ran all the faster.

Maria had no choice but to run after him. It was quite a job to keep up! For streets and streets they ran, before eventually Maria lost sight of him. She stopped and listened carefully, but could no longer hear his footsteps. Either he had got too far away or else he was hiding somewhere, hoping to shake her off.

'Where would he go?' Maria wondered. When Ryan was little, he often ran away -and he always ended up climbing. She scanned the skyline of the streets nearby. The highest building was an old church nearby in Main Street.

'That's where he'll be hiding' she guessed.

Maria walked quietly along Main Street. Then, right next to the church she stopped and looked up at the roof. Sure enough, there he was.

'Ryan, come on down! Where were you going anyway?'

Ryan didn't really know the answer to that himself. In the back of his mind there was some daft notion that Nick might live near the hospital, and that maybe if he headed that way, he might run into him again. But by the time he climbed onto the church roof, he was tired of running.

'Ryan, will you come down?' Maria asked him.

'No, go away' he answered.

'Tell me why you were running away'

'No'

'OK then. I'll just stay here till you come down'

Maria knew Ryan could be very stubborn.

'But I can be just as stubborn' she thought to herself. 'I won't waste my breath trying to persuade him. I'll just wait here. He'll have to come down some time'

Ryan, on the other hand, decided he was not coming down until she went away. So the scene was set for a real battle of wills!

Every now and then Maria would call up

'I'm still waiting, Ryan. I'm not going away'

Both of them were getting cold and tired, but still neither of them would admit it.

'I wish to heavens I could understand Ryan' Maria thought as she hunched against the church wall. 'He's my own brother, but he acts so weird at times'

Suddenly she remembered the red notebook and took it out from her inside pocket, where it had been since she lifted from Ryan's room. What should she do with it? He had written 'Important Lists-PRIVATE' across the front, and she knew how fussy he was about things like that. Maybe she could use it to bribe him down?

No, she thought. If Ryan knew she had his private notebook, he would jump down, snatch it from her and run off again. She would sneak a look inside. Maybe it would give her some clues about what was going on!

So she crept round the side of the church, to a spot under a streetlight and began to read.

Maria could hardly believe what she was reading

.....Ryan was worried he would be sent to 'Freak School'

..... He was *seriously* worried that Danny was going to murder him? How on earth could he believe something like that?

.....He was worried about getting ear injury, just because dad said he could be thrown out on his ear! How could anyone misunderstand a remark like that?

.....He had prepared a Masterplan and a Class List to help him make friends?.... Maria felt tears coming into her eyes.

.....And he was thinking of joining the *Kelly Gang* - to protect him from Danny, of all things? The idea was a joke.

But as she read on she realised it was not funny at all. Nick Kelly had obviously got involved with Ryan. She had no idea why, but she knew he must have been up to no good. Maria had heard a lot about Nick Kelly, and none of it was good. Her heart missed a beat. She could only guess what had gone on between them, but this had to be something to do with the Belmont Burglaries. Nick Kelly must have set Ryan up!

Even more amazing to Maria was the fact that Ryan needed to make out one of his lists to help him work out who he could trust. And that he imagined that *Nick Kelly* was going to help him.

Maria's heart was racing by now. She ran back inside the church grounds.

'Ryan!' she called urgently. 'I've read your private notebook. I'm sorry. I know I shouldn't have, but I just had to. I know about Nick Kelly now. Look, this is urgent. I'm going to help you, but you'll have to give me the whole story'

Normally the idea of someone reading his Secret Journal would have made Ryan very angry. But in a strange way he felt relieved that at last someone else knew.

'Can you help me find Nick?' he called down, hopefully.

'Find Nick?' she repeated, amazed. 'Ryan, there are some things you don't understand'

Maria took a deep breath. She knew what she was about to tell Ryan was going to be hurt him, because to Ryan, Nick was his friend - the person who could help clear his name. And Maria knew what Ryan was like. Once he made his mind up about a person, it was very hard for him to change it. The only way to get through to him was to be very blunt.

'Look Ryan' she began. 'I know this is hard for you to take in, but Nick Kelly is a vicious criminal. If he made you think he was your friend, he has deceived you. I don't know exactly what went on. I just know Nick Kelly must have set you up'

Ryan said nothing.

'What was the Key Game, Ryan?' she persisted.

He didn't answer, so she took a guess.

'Ryan, did he use you because of how well you can climb? Did you get keys for him or something? -Because if so, he has used them to steal from a lot of homes. It's so obvious, Ryan. Nick Kelly is the Belmont Burglar, Ryan. Not you!'

Ryan could hardly believe what he was hearing.

'You must be wrong' he said.

'I'm not wrong, Ryan, believe me. And Nick Kelly must have attacked Kev as well'

When he heard that, Ryan climbed down from the roof, in a state of shock. It was hard to take in what Maria was saying, but in his heart, somehow he knew she was right. It made perfect sense. Nick must have somehow copied the keys. Why on earth had he not been able to work all this out for himself? He must be the stupidest person alive.

'We need to go to the Police' said Maria.

'No' said Ryan.

'What do you mean NO?'

'Please don't tell anyone, Maria' he pleaded. 'Not yet anyway'

Maria wasn't sure it was a good idea to keep something like this to themselves, but she could see it meant a lot to Ryan. And Dad had said the Court Case could take months and months anyway, so she supposed there was no great urgency.

'All right then – but just for a while though' she agreed.

'You won't even tell Mum or Dad?'

'Suppose so'

'Promise, Maria?'

'OK then!' she said reluctantly, 'as long as you tell me everything you know'

Ryan agreed, and as they walked home together, for the first time he began to tell her about what had gone on.

Luckily they managed to sneak back into the house without being missed.

Chapter 16

'ICEBERGER'
SYNDROME

When Ryan realised that Nick had deceived him, it was a real shock. But something good came out of it as well. It made him think about Maria in a new light. He thought about the fact that she had bothered to run after him in the middle of the night - and the fact that she believed in him, even when all the evidence was stacked against him.

Every cloud has a silver lining, as they say, and it was certainly true here - because for the first time, Ryan realised at a deep level that his sister loved him. Which was a silver lining indeed!

Maria longed to tell her parents what she knew, but she didn't want to break her promise.

'We can't keep all this to ourselves forever' she kept reminding Ryan. 'What if the Police take you to court?'

'Dad said that could take ages. Don't say anything yet'

'OK then – but why?'

'I don't want Mum and Dad knowing how stupid I was'

'They're going to have to know some time'

'Maybe – but not yet'

A piece of great news came through that evening. Maria looked in on Ryan just before he went to sleep to tell him.

'Kev Shepherd has come out of his coma'

Ryan was delighted.

'He has to stay in hospital for a few more days' Maria told him. 'But it looks like he will make a full recovery!'

All of a sudden Ryan's face fell.

'What's wrong, Ryan?'

'It's all my fault, isn't it? None of this would have happened if I hadn't been so stupid'

'Stop saying you're stupid'

'But I am stupid'

Maria sensed that he was very troubled.

'Ryan, what is it?'

'Tell me the truth, Maria. Do you think there's something wrong with me?'

'No way!'

'So how come I'm always in trouble then? How come I've no friends? And I have such problems knowing who to trust?'

'OK, you are different to most people, Ryan. But that doesn't mean there's something *wrong* with you'

'Mum and Dad think there's something wrong with me'

'I'm sure they don't, Ryan. Now go on to sleep'

But of course Ryan couldn't sleep. He lay awake worrying about what Maria had said. He supposed she was right. He was going to have to tell Mum and Dad some time, but he dreaded it. Maria had said they would be delighted when they found out their son was not the Belmont Burglar. That was all very well, but they were still going to have a son who was stupid....a son who caused nothing but problems for people.... a son who must have something wrong with him.

It was about half past midnight when eventually Ryan made up his mind. He would have to tell his parents the truth. He could hear the faint drone of their voices in the living room, so he knew they were still up.

Nervously, he went downstairs. For a few moments he stopped at the living room door, trying to pluck up his courage. Then just as he was about to give a knock, he couldn't help hearing his own name being mentioned. And what he heard sent a chill through his bones.

'Yes, I know Ryan's always been different' Mum was saying, 'but this is still hard to take in'

Dad's voice was quieter, so Ryan could only make out Mum's side of the conversation properly.

'Yes. I suppose it does explain a lot' she said a moment later, in response to something Dad said.

Then he heard her say

'That's true. We couldn't have a more expert opinion'

Ryan pressed his ear to the door, trying to hear what Dad was saying, but he could only make out a few words. When he heard him use the words 'Ryan's diagnosis', his heart missed a beat.

'So I was right, he thought sadly. 'I have something wrong with me'

He strained his ears, hoping he might hear the name of his illness.

'I can hardly believe it' he heard his Dad saying. 'Imagine Ryan having Iceberger Syndrome'

Ryan had heard enough. He went slowly back to bed,

the colour drained from his face. What he had heard
confirmed his worst fears. He tried to piece it all together
in his mind. Certain words played over in his head - the
word 'diagnosis' for example. To Ryan, diagnosis meant
illness. He wondered how ill he was. Maybe it was a
mental illness. That might explain why he could be so
stupid at times. But then again he had heard the word
'syndrome' too. 'Syndrome' sounded more like a physical
illness. Perhaps he was going to die soon!

The other word that kept replaying in Ryan's head
was one that puzzled him. It was the word 'Iceberger'.
He had heard Dad say he had 'Iceberger Syndrome'. That
sounded awful. Trust him to have an illness with a weird
name like 'Iceberger Syndrome'! He crept out of bed and
switched on his laptop. Surely he was entitled to find out
more about the thing that was wrong with him. So he
performed a search under 'Iceberger Syndrome'.

Much to his disappointment, he could find nothing
on the internet that made any sense, so he was left to use
his imagination. Iceberger Syndrome must be very rare,
he decided. And it must be something to do with icebergs
too. All Ryan knew about icebergs was that they could be
very dangerous. Dad had told him once that only 10%
of an iceberg showed above the water line, and because of
that but they could do a lot of damage. An iceberg caused
the Titanic to sink and kill hundreds of people.

The more he thought about it, the more fearful Ryan
became. It sounded like Iceberger Syndrome was a really
dangerous disease.

Chapter 17

TRYING TO MAKE
AMENDS

The next morning was Saturday, but Ryan got up early anyway. He waited anxiously to see if Mum or Dad would mention 'Iceberger Syndrome'. They didn't, which made Ryan imagine the worst. My illness must be very serious, he thought, if they don't even want to tell me about it. He wondered if Maria and Danny knew too. Maybe everyone except me knows, he thought ruefully, that I'm going to die.

'Maria' he asked. 'Would you take me to the hospital to visit Kevin this morning?'

'You know Mum and Dad wouldn't like it, Ryan'

'They don't need to know. They didn't know the last time'

'Well, OK then' she said reluctantly.

So the two of them took the bus to the hospital like they did before. And this time things went a lot better. Kev had no visitors when they arrived, but the nurses allowed them a very short visit. It was great to see Kev awake and looking well, though he still had no memory about the assault.

After the visit, Ryan decided to tell Maria what he had in mind.

'Remember the last time we came here?' he said, as they left the Ward 15.

'As if I could forget!' she smiled.

'Well, the reason I did a runner that day was that I thought I saw Nick Kelly'

'Are you sure?

'No, but it could have been him'

'Gosh, Ryan!' she said, shocked. 'If Nick Kelly's hanging around, Kev could be in danger again'

'I know' agreed Ryan. 'But I've got a plan'

'A plan?'

'I want to hang around the hospital today and keep a look out. If I see him again, then we'll know for sure'

'Ryan, that's crazy!'

'Don't worry, I'll be careful'

'No way!'

'But I have to, Maria. This whole thing is my fault. It's up to me to make amends'

'Ryan, this is a matter for the Police. If Nick Kelly's about, it could be dangerous. You could get yourself killed'

Ryan took a deep breath and decided to tell her.

'You don't need to worry about me being killed'

'Of course I'll worry!'

'There's no point. I'm going to die anyway'

'What are you on about?' she said, laughing.

Then she looked at Ryan's face and realised he was perfectly serious.

'Honestly. I overheard Mum and Dad talking about it last night. I've got a serious disease'

'What is it?' said Maria, shocked. 'They didn't tell me'

'It's something called Iceberger Syndrome'

Maria gasped.

'What's that?'

'I think it's very rare' he said.

Maria's eyes were filling up with tears.

'Oh, Ryan. I'm so sorry' she said.

'So will you let me do his my way?'

'What about if I stay at the hospital with you?'

'No, I want to do this on my own. I owe it to Kevin'

It took quite a bit more argument and persuasion but in the end Maria agreed.

'OK' she said, 'I'll go home and make up a cover story to stop Mum and Dad worrying about you. I suppose you can't come to much harm in broad daylight. As long as you promise to keep your distance if you do see Nick Kelly'

'OK'

'And remember to keep your mobile phone on. Ring me right away if there are any problems'

After Maria left, Ryan found a bench in a remote corner to use as a look out. He had a good view from there of the hospital gates. For over an hour he sat, carefully watching people as they came in and out. No sign of Nick. Then at about 2.30, he saw him. He was walking swiftly in Ryan's direction!

Ryan held his breath, but Nick walked straight by without even a glance. It was Nick all right. Ryan had no doubt now. He watched as Nick headed straight in the direction of Ward 15. Then quietly, he got up and followed him from a safe distance.

At the entrance to Ward 15, Nick stopped and spoke to the nurse. Ryan went as close as he dared and then stopped at a notice board. Pretending to read the notices, he strained his ears.

'You're Kevin Shepherd's uncle?' the nurse was saying. 'Yes, he's much better today…. Still no memory of what happened to him though, poor kid. Come on and I'll take you in to see him'

'That would be great' answered Nick. He made as if to walk after her into the ward. Then he stopped and banged his forehead with the heel of his hand.

'I knew I'd forgotten something!' he exclaimed. 'I bought some chocolate for him and I've left it in the car. I'll be back with it shortly'

And he turned back towards the entrance with a cheery wave.

Ryan was incensed. What a liar! He thought to himself. Kevin's uncle indeed! Ryan didn't know what Nick was up to. But clearly Kevin was in danger and Ryan felt he had to do something.

He followed Nick out of the hospital, again keeping a safe distance. They followed the same route as the previous day, but this time Nick had no idea he was being followed, so he made no effort to shake Ryan off. Eventually they turned into a street full of high-rise flats.

Ryan managed to see which block Nick entered, but he was not close enough to know which flat he had gone to, or even which floor. After waiting a few minutes, he wandered round behind the block, to a place where he could not easily be seen. Then he hoisted himself up onto a ledge and began to scale the building. Climbing round the sides, he peeped carefully through as many back windows as he could, until at last he found the flat that Nick was in. It was on the 5th floor.

Hunched on the windowsill, Ryan watched Nick as

he talked on the phone for a few minutes. Then he put the phone down and walked back towards the hall. The front door banged behind him as he left the flat.

'What a stroke of luck' thought Ryan. 'That phone call must have been something urgent that he had to go out and see to'

This was his only chance -he had to get inside. The window of the bedroom right next to him was open just a crack. Slowly and carefully, he eased it open fully and climbed in.

Ryan didn't want to stay in the flat one more moment than was necessary, so he began his search right away. If only he could find all those things that Nick had stolen! They were probably hidden in this flat, Ryan thought, and if so maybe he could find them.

Heart pounding, he began to hunt around anywhere he could think of – under beds, in drawers, cupboards, shelves. At last he found what he was looking for! They were in a sideboard in the living room – two plastic bags bunged full of credit cards, wallets, bundles of cash and jewellery. Wait till Maria sees all this, he thought, excited!

A sudden noise made him stop what he was doing. It was the sound of a key turning in the door. Oh, no, he thought. It must be Nick coming back!

There was no time for Ryan to climb out. He shoved the sideboard door closed and looked around furiously for somewhere to hide. The only place he could spot was behind a sofa, which was sitting diagonally across the corner of the room. He just made it behind this with his two bags of 'loot' before the living room door opened.

Nick had only stepped out for a moment. He had just forgotten to pick up the mail from his mailbox on his way by, so he was back in the flat in minutes. He came in and turned on the TV. Then he settled down on the sofa to watch it, unaware that Ryan was hiding only a few feet behind him.

Hunched down, stock still, Ryan was only too aware of the danger he was in. At the next commercial break, Nick went into the kitchen to put the kettle on. Quickly Ryan pulled out his mobile phone. He tried to phone Maria, but could hardly get his hands to stop shaking. At last her number was ringing. But before she answered it, Ryan could hear Nick coming back into the room.

Maria might try to ring him back now, he realised. He would have to turn the phone off. And as he did so, he felt a chill run up his spine. Now Maria and he had no way of contacting each other.

Chapter 18

FAMILY MEETING

On her way home from the hospital, Maria wondered had she done the right thing, leaving Ryan on his own like that. Maybe it was a stupid thing to do, and she should have insisted on staying with him. But the news he had told her about his health had given her such a shock that she couldn't think straight. And Ryan was very hard to argue with when he got something into his head!

He'll be OK, she reassured herself. Even if it was Nick Kelly that he saw the last time he was here, what are the chances that he'll see him again today? And even if he does, he knows to keep well away from him. Plus he's got his mobile phone, so he can let me know if there are any problems. I'm sure he'll come to no harm, she reassured herself.

All she had to do now was think of a cover story to tell Mum and Dad. She decided to say she they had been at the library, and Ryan would make his own way home later. But she hoped they wouldn't ask.

As it happened, it was the first thing Dad asked as soon as she walked in the door.

'Where's Ryan?'

'He's staying on at the library' she said convincingly. 'He's going to get a later bus home'

She was relieved when he didn't question her any further.

'OK. You're just in time for dinner' he said.

There was very little talking done over dinner. As

usual, it was as if no one knew what to say to each other these days. Afterwards each of them piled their dishes at the sink and Mum busied herself clearing the table.

'Hold on, everyone' Dad said out of the blue. 'We all need to sit down and talk'

Mum seemed taken aback.

'No, Mike. Not now'

'Yes, now' he retorted. 'We can't go on like this as a family. There's no point in not talking about things when they need talking about'

Mum sighed. She knew when Dad meant business.

'Come on, Danny and Maria' she said. 'Sit down. It looks like we're going to have a Family Meeting'

Maria's heart missed a beat. She had a feeling she knew what this was about. Mum and Dad were going to tell them that Ryan was terminally ill.

'But Ryan's not here' she protested. 'How can it be a Family Meeting without Ryan?

'What do you think, stupid?' snarled Danny. 'The meeting is to *talk* about Ryan. You can't go on for ever not mentioning it when you've got a real live *thief* in the family'

'He's *not* a thief' yelled Maria.

'Calm down, you two' said Dad. 'And I want no more insults from you, Danny. Ryan's your brother don't forget. But you're right....there are some things we need to talk before Ryan comes back'

'It's not an insult' protested Danny. 'It's the truth. Ryan's the Belmont Burglar. We all know it. Before long the whole school will know as well'

'Look, we're not here to talk about the Belmont

Burglar' said Mum.

'So what are we here to talk about then?' he asked.

Mum and Dad looked at each other, as if each wanted the other to begin.

'This is a bit hard to explain' Dad began.

'It's OK, Dad' interrupted Maria, with tears in her eyes. 'I know what you're going to tell us'

'You do?' said Mum, amazed.

'Yes'

'How do you know?'

'Ryan told me'

Dad looked at her, puzzled.

'What did he tell you, Maria?'

'He overheard the two of you talking last night'

'So he knows?'

'Yes'

'And he understands what it means?'

'Pretty well – though he doesn't know how long he's got'

'How long he's got?' repeated Mum. 'Got to what?'

'To live' said Maria sadly.

At this point even Danny seemed shocked.

'No way!' he said. 'You mean Ryan is dying?'

Everyone ignored him.

'Poor lad' said Mum quietly. 'What on earth does he think he overheard?'

'That he's got a rare disease called Icebreaker Syndrome….. No, I mean Iceberger Syndrome. That was it'

It was clear to Mum and Dad that the time was right for

them to be as honest and clear as they could to Maria and Danny.

'No' Dad told them. 'Ryan does not have a life threatening illness. We won't know for certain until he can get a full assessment, but it does look like he has Asperger Syndrome'

'What's Asperger Syndrome?' asked Maria.

'Well, it's not an illness anyway' said Dad.

'So what is it then?'

'Well, your Mum and I are only learning about it ourselves, so it's hard to explain. But it seems to me that it's more like a different way of being'

'Have you ever heard of autism?' asked Mum.

'A bit' said Maria.

'Well, it seems to be related to autism in some way. Which would explain why Ryan finds it so hard to relate to people'

'So he's not dying then?' Danny asked.

'Try not to sound so disappointed, Danny!' said Maria kicking out at him under the table.

'That was sore!' he protested. 'Dad, she just kicked me, did you see that?'

Again everyone ignored Danny.

'Asperger Syndrome certainly seems to explain a lot of Ryan's difficulties' said Mum.

'And his strengths' added Dad.

'That's right. Here, I have some information the two of you could read if you like' she said passing some leaflets to them.

Danny didn't take much interest, but Maria took one.

'This all sounds like Ryan OK' she said as she began

to read. 'It says here that people with Asperger Syndrome often have unusual ways of thinking and remembering things…. Ryan's got an amazing memory sometimes'

'Does it say they make good burglars as well?' asked Danny.

No one bothered to answer him.

'Remember, it's up to us to tell Ryan about this. Not either of you' Mum warned. 'We'll probably talk to him later today. But it's better that we've put you two in the picture before we do'

Maria took all the leaflets and books she could get from Mum and Dad to her room and started to read. It was all very interesting! She couldn't wait to tell Ryan that he wasn't dying after all. Not only that, but that there was an explanation for the things he found so difficult. Most people with Asperger Syndrome had problems like his, and a lot of them were really intelligent! And there were ways to make life better for him as well.

She had been so excited in fact that she left her phone downstairs. So when Ryan phoned her from behind Nick's sofa, she didn't even hear the phone ringing.

Mum put her head round the bedroom door later.

'What time did you say Ryan was coming home at?' she asked. 'I thought the library closed at 5.00 on Saturday'

Maria had got so involved in her reading that she didn't realise it was so late. But she didn't want to get herself or Ryan into trouble.

'No, it's open late tonight' she lied. 'He'll probably not be long now'

'I see you're still reading about Asperger Syndrome'

'Yes, it's helping me understand Ryan so much. How did you find out about it?'

'It was Jim Shepherd actually. It turns out that he is a world-renowned expert in Asperger Syndrome…. He told us what happened when he met Ryan in the hospital'

'You mean he was able to tell Ryan had Asperger Syndrome just from meeting him for two seconds?

'No' she said laughing. 'Apparently he first met Ryan some time before that. And Kev had told him a lot about Ryan as well. He has now interviewed us - and spoken to his doctors and his teachers. From all that he's learned about Ryan, he seems pretty convinced he has Asperger Syndrome. He just needs to assess Ryan in person to confirm it'

'Do you think Ryan will be pleased when he finds out?'

'Well, I'm sure he will. The diagnosis will help him in his Court case. Hopefully, the judge will make allowances when he is sentencing him'

'Mum, you're talking as if Ryan really is the Belmont Burglar. He's not, you know!'

Mum smiled, but Maria could tell she didn't believe her. Just wait till she hears the whole story about Nick Kelly, thought Maria. She wanted to tell her right then, but she had promised Ryan that she wouldn't. Gosh, there would be so much to talk to Ryan about when he got home. Whenever that would be! He hadn't phoned her all day, so she supposed he must be OK.

Then in a flash she realised – she'd left her phone downstairs. He could have been ringing all day long and she mightn't have heard! She flew down and grabbed it.

One missed call and one message. Yes, the missed call was from him. And the message too. Oh dear, she thought. I hope he got the bus OK.

But when she read the message her blood ran cold.

'Climbed in Nick's window' it read *'hiding behind sofa. must keep phone off. will escape when i can. Wait 4me at hosp gates'*

Chapter 19

PROFESSOR JAMES

Maria didn't waste another moment. She ran straight for the front door, pulling on her jacket as she went.

'Where are you going?' asked Mum.

'Out!' she replied, pulling the door closed behind her.

'Teenagers!' Mum tutted to herself. 'Honestly, they can be so rude at times!'

Luckily Maria just managed to catch a bus, but the journey seemed to take forever.

'Hurry up! Hurry up!' she muttered under her breath, each time they slowed down or stopped at traffic lights.

She kept trying Ryan's phone, but it was still switched off. That probably meant he was still trapped at Nick's. And it was a few hours now since he had left the message.

As she expected, Ryan was not at the hospital gates when she arrived. Suddenly she knew what to do. She ran for Ward 15, looking frantically for Jim Shepherd. Thank heavens he was there - at his grandson's side as usual.

'Jim! Jim!' she called urgently.

Jim Shepherd looked up from the paper he was reading before getting up to talk to her. Kevin was sound asleep, so they talked in the corridor.

'Jim, you have to help' she said urgently. 'Mum and Dad told me about Ryan having Asperger Syndrome. You're an expert. You must know what to do'

'Calm down, Maria' said Jim. 'What's all this about?'

'Ryan's in danger' she said, agitated. 'I'd no idea he'd go and break into Nick Kelly's flat. Who knows what he'll do next?'

'Ryan's broken in to Nick Kelly's flat?' repeated Jim, alarmed.

'Yes, and he's trapped there now. And I don't know where Nick Kelly lives. And I can't even get in touch with Ryan'

There must have been something about saying it all out loud, but suddenly Maria realised the seriousness of the danger that Ryan was in, and she burst into floods of tears.

It took some time for Jim to get her to calm down enough, but eventually he managed to hear the whole story. He was aghast to hear that Nick had been hanging round the hospital. There was no knowing what he was planning to do, but it was clear Kevin could be in danger too.

'And you're saying the Police know nothing of all this?' he checked.

'No. Mum and Dad don't even know. Ryan didn't want them to think he was stupid. He wanted to handle it his own way'

'I'm sure I don't have to tell you this, Maria, but the Police will have to be told now'

'I suppose so' she said heavily. 'It's just that I promised Ryan…'

'Well, you can blame me if you like' he said 'but I'm heading for the Station right away. Do you want to come with me?'

'I can't. Ryan asked me to wait for him at the hospital gates'

'I understand. Just don't go doing anything silly now'

As he strode off, he lifted his mobile phone.

'This is Professor James Shepherd here' Maria heard him say. 'I need to speak urgently to the Police Detective dealing with the case against young Ryan Gillespie'

Standing at the hospital gates, Maria was starting to get more and more drenched. It had begun to rain heavily, but she didn't dare to move even a short distance to take shelter in case Ryan suddenly showed up. However there was little chance of that at the moment. Nick Kelly had settled down to watch a film, and Ryan was still stuck behind his sofa, anxiously awaiting his chance to escape.

It was a short time later, when the doorbell rang, that Ryan decided to take his chance. He knew that if he didn't he could end up trapped there all night. So the moment Nick stepped into the hall to go to the front door, Ryan made his move. He grabbed the plastic bags containing the stolen goods, made a run for it towards the bedroom and climbed out of the window as quickly and quietly as he could

......But not quietly enough, as he soon found out.

'What's that?' Stevie asked as he came in.

'What?'

'That noise...Is someone in your room, Nick?' he asked, puzzled.

'Don't think so' said Nick. But he opened the bedroom door just to check, and as he did he caught a glimpse of Ryan on the windowsill, just before he slipped out of sight.

'It's that freak kid' he explained. 'He was following me yesterday. Must have been trying to climb in the window. Don't worry. I'll be waiting for him next time he shows up'

Unfortunately in his rush, Ryan had dropped a necklace out of one of the bags. Stevie noticed it as he entered the living room and went straight to the sideboard and opened it.

'You reckon he was trying to get in, do you?' he said. 'Looks to me like he's been in already. And he's lifted the lot!'

Nick had never been more angry in his life. There was no way that little freak would get away with it, he thought. He couldn't have got very far. Nick dashed to the door, flew down the steps three at a time and ran out of the building – just quickly enough to catch a glimpse of Ryan before he turned into the next street.

Within moments Ryan realised he was being chased. He held tightly onto his plastic bags and kept running through the rain. But no matter how fast he ran, he couldn't shake Nick off. Ryan knew where he was heading. He wanted to get to the hospital gates, because he had asked Maria to wait for him there. But he hadn't a clue what he would do when he got there if he hadn't shaken Nick Kelly off by that time.

When at last Maria saw Ryan running along the far side of the street at full speed, she heaved a sigh of relief.

'Ryan! Thank heavens you're safe' she called over.

But Ryan just ran straight on, without a glance across, and within moments she knew why. He was being chased.

At that exact moment she heard sirens and a Police Car pulled up next to her. Kevin's grandfather got out with a couple of Police Officers.

'You've just missed them' she yelled. 'Ryan ran past a moment ago with a man chasing after him. They went that way'

At once the Policemen ran off in the direction she pointed.

'Don't worry, Maria. The Police Officers will find them' Jim reassured her. 'And I've contacted your parents too. They'll be here shortly'

And sure enough, within five minutes, the Policemen walked back. Nick Kelly was with them, wearing a pair of handcuffs. It had turned out to be quite a chase, and in the end it had taken both of the officers to bring Nick Kelly to the ground and physically restrain him.

Ryan walked alongside, looking delighted with himself. He was still carrying his plastic bags.

'Look, Maria' he said eagerly. 'I got the stolen goods back.... And the Police have caught the *real* Belmont Burglar now'

'Thanks to you, Ryan' said one of the Policemen. 'You're a brave young man, aren't you?'

Proudly Ryan handed over his two plastic bags to the Police Officer. Nick Kelly looked furious, but he said nothing as he was bundled into the back of the Police Car.

Kevin's grandfather shook Ryan warmly by the hand.

'And thanks to you, Ryan, I know my grandson will

be safe now too. Hopefully Nick Kelly will stay behind bars for a very long time'

Maria couldn't resist giving Ryan a hug.

'Ryan, if only you knew how worried I've been about you!'

'What do you think Mum and Dad will say?' asked Ryan.

Just at that she saw their car approaching.

'Looks like we're about to find out' said Maria smiling.

Then she turned to Ryan.

'Ryan, you know who this is, don't you?'

'Yeah. You're Kevin's grandfather, aren't you?' said Ryan.

'That's right' he replied. 'But let me introduce myself properly. I am Professor James Shepherd'

'You're a professor?' said Ryan, impressed.

'I am indeed. I am a professor of psychology, specialising in the field of Asperger Syndrome'

Chapter 20

I'M NOT A SWAN!

'You should have been there' Maria said excitedly, as she and Ryan bundled into Mum and Dad's car. 'Ryan was like a real hero. He went flying down the street at about hundred miles an hour with Nick Kelly on his heels…'

'I'm so glad you're OK, Ryan' said Mum, with tears in her eyes, for by now Jim Shepherd had explained everything to them. 'And listen, son. I just want you to know you're not dying or anything like that at all. So get that idea right out of your head!'

'…And he got all the stolen stuff back as well' Maria went on. 'I was so proud of him that I could have cried'

'I think I'll go on to bed' Ryan said, the moment they got home. And he went straight to his room.

'Oh well' Mum said 'I suppose he's very tired'

But Maria knew he had something on his mind, and she had a good idea what it might be.

The two of them talked about it later.

'Mum said I'm not dying' he told her. 'But I'm sure she's wrong'

'She's right. Look, they told me. You've got *Asperger* Syndrome. Not *Iceberger* Syndrome. It's not even an illness'

'How do you know?'

'I've been reading all about it' she said.

'What is Asperger Syndrome then?'

'I think Mum and Dad are going to talk to you about it tomorrow, but I'll tell you what. Here's all the stuff I've

137

been reading. You can have a look for yourself'

'Thanks' said Ryan, taking a pile of papers and books from her.

'I'll come back in a while and see what you think' she said, smiling.

Before long Ryan had read just about everything Maria gave him. Then he switched on his laptop and performed a search. This time he searched under the correct name - Asperger Syndrome, not Iceberger Syndrome. Some people just called it Aspergers or even A.S. for short. And Maria was right, he concluded. It's not an illness. It's really more like a different way of being.

He soon began to find links to lots of people all round the world who had Asperger Syndrome too - people who had difficulties very similar to his. Lots of them were really bright, interesting people. Some of them liked to call themselves 'Aspies'. Ryan thought that was cool. And lots of them hated school too!

'Well' said Maria later 'did you read it?'

'Yes' he said, smiling. 'I think I must be an Aspie, Maria'

'I think so too. Though you still have to get a proper assessment'

The next day, Ryan went to Mum and Dad himself.

'Maria let me read a lot of stuff about Asperger Syndrome' he volunteered. 'So when can I see Professor James for a proper assessment?'

Mum and Dad were taken aback.

'Well, he's coming here today' Mum said.

The assessment took place over the next few days. Hours

and hours of questions and tests left Ryan exhausted, but he never seemed to run out of questions to ask Jim (or Professor James as he liked to call him). He was determined to find out all he could about Asperger Syndrome and how it might affect him.

At the end of the process, Professor James was able to confirm to Ryan what he had suspected all along.

'Congratulations!' he joked. 'You do have Asperger Syndrome'

Ryan seemed very pleased.

'Dad said you knew from the start' Ryan said.

'I certainly suspected it' agreed Professor James. 'Ever since the day you returned my hat to me'

'Returned your hat to you?' repeated Ryan, puzzled.

'Do you not remember? It was one windy day'

Ryan remembered chasing an old man's hat one time. It was the same day that he had first met Nick Kelly.

'Oh, was that you?'

'It was indeed' said Professor James. 'And I've been keeping an eye on you ever since'

'You have?'

'Yes. My grandson, Kevin and I do talk about things, you know!' he laughed.

It was a while since Ryan had written in his Secret Journal. But when the Police gave him back his Cantadora Pen, he decided it was time he started a new list. He was certainly learning a lot these days so there was plenty to write about:

~~~~~~

Learning about Asperger Syndrome

List of important things I have found out so far about people who have Asperger Syndrome

1. *They may communicate differently to other people.*

2. *They are usually more honest than other people.*

3. *They usually mean what they say. (You can't assume that other people mean what they say. For example, when Danny said he was going to kill me, he didn't mean it. He just wanted to frighten me)*

4. *Sometimes they take things literally. (Other people use words in strange ways. Like when Dad said I would be thrown out of school on my ear, it was really nothing to do with my ear!)*

5. *Other times people with Asperger Syndrome can be very funny because they take things literally just for a joke.*

6. *They may think and learn differently to other people. Their brains and memories work differently. But schools don't understand this.*

7. *They may get more anxious than other people and have nervous habits because of this (like my Tooth Tapping)*

8. *They can get very focussed on things – (like I do with my List Making)*

9. *They rarely do things just to be the same as everyone else. Other people do, so they find it difficult to cope with people who just like to do their own thing.*

10. *They may like to be on their own a lot.*

11. *They can often come across as rude and unfriendly,*

even though they don't mean to.
12. *They can find it very hard to fit in and make friends.*

Asperger Syndrome is not an illness. It is a different way of being. Lots of people with Asperger Syndrome are very intelligent and talented, and many famous people and original thinkers have Asperger Syndrome like me.

In the weeks and months after Ryan's diagnosis, a lot of things changed for him. He came to realise that he was far from stupid, and that he did not have something 'wrong' with him after all. He was not a freak - and there wasn't even any such thing as Freak School!

It was very interesting for him to find out about other people throughout the world who had Asperger Syndrome as well. One day Professor James came in to the school and gave a talk. He even brought in books written by people who had Asperger Syndrome. A lot of the other pupils were very interested in these and began to treat Ryan with a newfound respect.

Much to everyone's relief, Kev made a full recovery within a short time, except that he never got back any memory of what had happened that fateful evening when he was attacked. But when the other pupils heard the role Ryan had played in helping catch the Belmont Burglar, they looked on him as something of a hero - which made it easier for Kev to be his friend without being teased.

Things gradually became easier in the Gillespie home as well, with everyone seeming happier and more relaxed. Except Danny, as you can imagine! He hated all the fuss that was being made about Ryan. Shortly after his diagnosis, a reporter came to the door one day and Danny answered it.

'You must be Ryan' she cooed.

'No. I'm Danny'

'Oh, You're not the boy with Aspergers then?' she said, sounding disappointed.

'No' muttered Danny. 'I'll just get him for you'

And to make matters worse, there was an article in the local paper all about Ryan – how courageous he was in helping catch the Belmont Burglar. And how he had Asperger Syndrome as well. Danny was starting to get quite jealous. How come Ryan got Aspergers and he didn't. It wasn't fair!

The Cantadora continued to come to see Ryan for a long time to come.

'You seem happier these days, Ryan' she said to him one evening.

'You know, I think I understand more about hidden messages in stories now' he told her.

'Really?'

'Yes. Remember when you told me the story about The Sun and the Wind?'

'Yes'

'Well, you said the message was that people can be powerful, like the sun, without being forceful and mean'

'And now you can see that for yourself?'

'Yes. I always thought Danny was stronger than me, but I don't think so any more'

'Good for you!' she said.

'And another thing – the message in the Ugly

Duckling story. I thought it was silly, but it's not really'

'I told you that, Ryan!' she joked. 'Now repeat after me –*I am not an Ugly Duckling. I'm a beautiful swan!*'

Ryan burst into laughter.

'I am not an Ugly Duckling' he began. '…..But I'm not a beautiful swan either…. I've just got ASPERGER SYNDROME!'

About the Author

Brenda Boyd is the author of the highly acclaimed 'Parenting a Child with Asperger Syndrome'. She is in a unique position to understand Asperger Syndrome, as she has a diagnosis of Aspergers herself, and works for the National Autistic Society.

She is the mother of Kenneth Hall, a teenager who has the condition, and is also author of the ever popular 'Asperger Syndrome, the Universe and Everything'. (both books published by Jessica Kingsley Publishers)

Brenda has been involved in the world of Asperger Syndrome for many years and regularly gives talks to promote understanding of this unique, intriguing, but often misunderstood condition.

She can be contacted at brenda.boyd@ntlworld.com

For further information about Asperger Syndrome, please contact the National Autistic Society on www.nas.org.uk

Printed in the United Kingdom
by Lightning Source UK Ltd.
121006UK00001B/193-210